Oriental Gardens

Oriental

Norah Titley
and Frances Wood

THE BRITISH LIBRARY

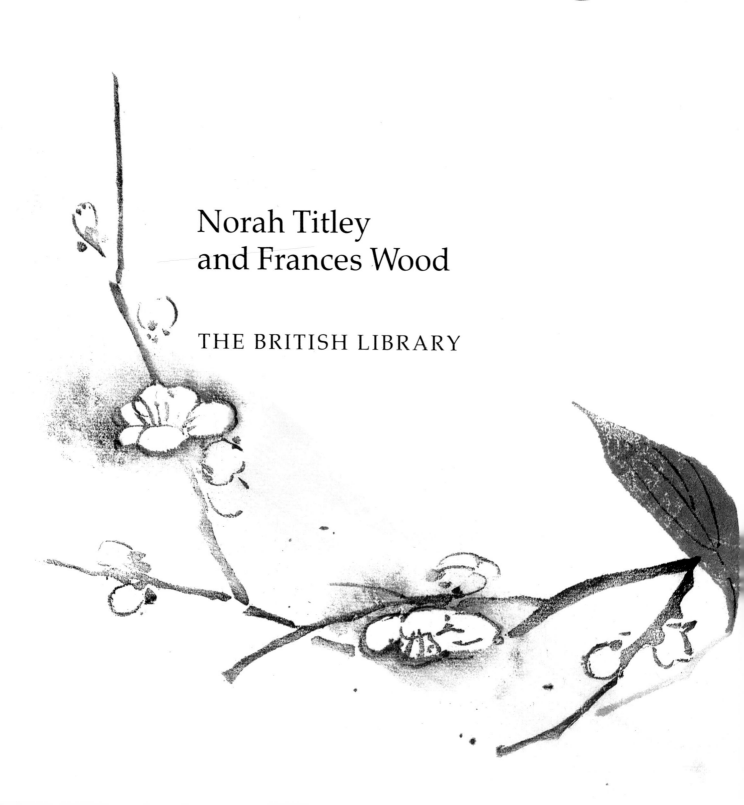

Gardens

HALF-TITLE PAGE
Detail from *Chikuzan teizoden* (How to make mountains and gardens)
Japanese woodblock print, 1795

TITLE PAGE
Winter-flowering narcissus, camellia and prunus, from *Jie zi yuan hua juan*
(Colour prints from the Mustard Seed Garden painting manual)
Chinese coloured woodblock print, *c*.1679–1791

THIS PAGE
From Akisato Rito's *Ishugumi sono yaekiden* (Eight Methods of piling rocks
to create a garden); [*see* 107].

CONTENTS PAGE
Flowering trees; [*see* 70].

First published by The British Library
Great Russell Street, London WC1B 3DG

British Library Cataloguing in Publication Data

Titley, Norah M.
Oriental gardens
I. Title   II. Wood, Frances
III. British Library
712.6

ISBN 0–7123–0239–5 (cloth)
ISBN 0–7123–0262–x (paperback)

Designed by Gillian Greenwood
Typeset in Linotype Palatino by Nene Phototypesetters,
Northampton
Printed in Singapore by Tien Wah Press Limited

Contents

Introduction 7

Ottoman Turkey 11

Iran 25

India 45

China 70

Japan 100

Southeast Asia 121

Bibliography 126

Index 127

Introduction

Gardens have played a part in most of the world's great civilizations. For the inhabitants of Asia, they have long represented a refuge, whether from the stark landscape and baking heat of Persia or the bureaucratic cares of office in China. The landmass of Asia, repository of many of the plants that are now cultivated in the back gardens of the West, has, despite its natural barriers, served as a highway along which plants and ideas of garden design travelled to and fro. Europeans travelled to China in search of plants as early as the 16th century when the Portuguese first discovered rhubarb and camphor. Yet the movement of plants across Asia began far earlier: exotic edibles including grapes, pomegranates, walnuts, sesame and cucumber were imported to China from Central Asia and beyond as early as the Han dynasty (206 BC–AD 220). Of these, grapes and pomegranates, at least, were later grown as much for their attractive foliage and flowers as their economic significance. Later, the depiction of the early flowering prunus in the Chinese style occurs in Ottoman ceramics and Mughal miniatures, suggesting that the plant itself had been brought to the gardens of those areas. And though China is credited as the native home of some 80 per cent of European garden flowers, plants such as the tulip, introduced to Europe from Turkey in the 16th century, have made an indelible impression on European planting.

Links between the great civilizations of Asia are complex. The landmass is physically divided yet the Mongol empire stretched right across it in the 13th to 15th centuries, allowing the free movement of goods and ideas. The Mughal emperor Babur who reigned from 1526–30 was a descendant of the great Turkish conqueror Timur and of the second son of Ghenghis Khan who had begun the Mongol conquests. Mughal miniatures, which frequently depict gardens, illustrate the mixed heritage. Gardens are divided by waterways in the Persian style yet some of the flowers depicted, such as the prunus, are of Chinese origin and the style of painting owes much to both West and East Asia. The elevation of the art of garden design in Ottoman Turkey, Persia, Mughal India, China and Japan, forms another link; for the elite of all these, gardens were an essential aspect of private life. Whilst a Mughal emperor might spend his youth in conquest, the gardens that he saw as he swept across national barriers helped to form the gardens he created for himself. In China, government officials would complain of the sound of the bugle, calling them to work, for they would prefer to linger in the rustic seclusion of a tiny garden.

If the gardens of Asia can be thus linked in inspiration, their styles are vastly different. Climate determined the differences to a great extent though the differing local cultures also created different ideals. The fundamental contrast is between the geometric designs of Persia and India and the rugged 'natural' mountains and pools of the Far East. As the illustrations in this book reveal, the geometry of Persian and Mughal gardens allows a complete view of the garden from raised pavilions. Gardens were the settings for feasts, gatherings and clandestine meetings, flowered carpets spread on the ground and silken tents erected for the event, the whole scene laid out for the viewer in magical detail. Gardens were used similarly in the Far East but, when depicted in illustrated books and albums, the whole is rarely revealed; instead, a corner of the garden is shown, the rest hidden. A visitor to a Chinese or Japanese garden was similarly presented with a series of views, one hidden from the next. The Chinese and Japanese themselves compared their gardens to handscroll paintings which were gradually unfurled for visitors, revealing one scene after another. Later Japanese gardens, constricted by the fast growth of towns and cities, began to use the fixed viewpoint that characterizes many Near Eastern gardens. Their contents, however, were markedly different. Instead of the profusion of flowers between the regular water channels, a sombre grey and silver scene created from raked sand and irregularly disposed rocks, with only a hint of greenery, is laid out for the contemplation of visitors.

Illustrated books and albums from all corners of Asia are well represented in The British Library's collections. Many of them depict gardens, as the setting for the great epic poems of Turkey and Persia or the rambling novels of Japan and China. In their attention to detail, they represent an ideal source of information on garden design. Even in the Far East, where often it is only a corner of a garden that is glimpsed, these details convey the care with which corners of gardens or areas adjacent to houses were landscaped to provide a refreshing view from a verandah or pavilion. The depiction of landscaped gardens in Far Eastern books is supplemented by the number of garden design manuals that survive from the 13th century. Chinese manuals, such as Ji Cheng's 17th century *Yuan Ye* (The Craft of Gardens), not only lay out the details of construction of pavilions, rockeries, pools, paths and beds, but also convey the poetic ideal of the gentleman's rustic retreat. Later Japanese manuals concentrate on layout. Illustrations of tea-house gardens show each rock in a stepping-stone series carefully numbered, sometimes with measurements of the exact distance desired between each stone. Works such as these can still enable us to construct our own tea-house garden, with grass, stepping-stones and lanterns placed according to traditional principles, whilst the jewel-like colours of Near Eastern miniatures provide inspiration for planting, mixing brilliant blues and reds and shading the ground with dark trees.

GLOSSARY

Bonsai: the Japanese form of *pen cai* (*see* below), popular since the 17th century, producing smaller, spikier miniatures than the Chinese version.

Chahar Bagh: the 'four gardens' system of garden design which originated in Iran. Four water channels flow at right angles between flower-beds into a central pool.

Kiosks: Turkish garden pavilions.

Pen cai: a Chinese term literally meaning 'reared in pots' where the roots of plants are cut and their stems twisted to form miniatures.

Pen jing: a technique related to *pen cai*, literally 'pot scene'. Rocks and pebbles are set in water in earthenware dishes to form decorative 'mountain and lake' scenes.

Qanat: An Iranian system of irrigation dating back to the sixth century BC. Underground tunnels on different levels divert the water supply to where it is needed.

Yalis: Turkish summer dwellings.

Ottoman Turkey

In Turkey, the interest in flowers and gardens is evident from contemporary accounts of the earliest period of Ottoman rule up to the present day. Whether palace or private gardens or public parks, Turkish gardens have always been of a more haphazard design than the geometric layout of those in Iran and Mughal India, which serve as a refuge from the heat of summer. The *chahar bagh* or four gardens system of water channels at right angles to each other enclosing flower beds was not often employed in Ottoman gardens, the preference being for fountains and pools. In particular fountains were a feature not only of Ottoman gardens but of city and village streets. In different sizes and designs, they are to be met with everywhere and were used in garden kiosks (pavilions) in preference to water channels.

The Ottoman Sultan, Mehmed II, who conquered Constantinople (renamed Istanbul) in 1453, first made his capital at Adrianople (modern Edirne) and built a palace there surrounded by gardens and parkland. He moved his capital to Istanbul in 1457 and built the Topkapi Saraye (or palace) on its magnificent site. As at Edirne, he planned pleasure gardens round the palace which are still in evidence today although succeeding sultans altered them and added more kiosks and other buildings. Mehmed II was a practical gardener who delighted not only in planning gardens wherever he built palaces or mosques, but, according to contemporary accounts, actually working in them whenever he could spare time between his various campaigns. He founded the imperial cemetery at Bursa, where his own tomb dating back to 1451, together with ten others, is set in a rambling garden where roses are now grown.

The Topkapi Saraye had very extensive gardens in the 15th century, laid out with flower beds and trees of all kinds – cypress, planes, pines, willows and box amongst them – the whole area being surrounded by a high wall. The gardens originally covered a far larger area than they do today, extending to what is now the modern coast road running by the Sea of Marmara and including the Gülhâne Park on one side and extending to the Golden Horn on the other.

Istanbul, in contrast to the desert conditions suffered by Iran and India, has the advantage of its position on the shores of the Bosphorus,

2 *Decorative paper cut-outs of flowers in vases, an Ottoman speciality.* [Or. 13763D]

OPPOSITE
1 *Festivities and entertainments at the Sweet Waters of Europe (Kağithâne) in its heyday, depicted in a late 18th-century manuscript painting.* [Or. 7094, f. 7a]

the Sea of Marmara and the Golden Horn which provide relief from the worst of the summer heat. Sultans, nobles and eminent citizens built palaces and summer dwellings (*yalis*) at the water's edge, each with a garden that stretched up the slopes behind it. Evliya Çelebi in his *Narrative of Travels*[1] compiled in the 17th century, commented that if he were to describe minutely all the pleasure palaces, gardens, *yalis*, kiosks and walks in Istanbul, it would be a long work. Some of the old *yalis*, carefully restored, still stand on the shores, together with more modern buildings. These are best seen from the ferry boats which ply up and down the Bosphorus between the fishing villages, and to the Princes' Islands on the Sea of Marmara. Terraced gardens are laid out on the slopes behind the houses, reaching up to the natural area of trees and shrubs where paths ramble among umbrella pines, Judas trees, cypresses, and other indigenous trees.

Evliya Çelebi, writing of the gardens and houses at the village of Beşiktaş down the Bosphorus, noted that 'there were no less than a hundred and sixty gardens, every one like a paradise, fragrant of roses, narcissus and oderiferous [*sic*] herbs'. A tulip festival is held every April above Emirğan while Büyükada, the largest of the Princes' Islands, still has beautiful 19th-century wooden houses with their original gardens. These gardens, with their shady paths, terraced borders, fountains and kiosks provided colour, coolness and privacy.

Charles White,[2] writing in the mid-19th century, described private gardens in the vicinity of the Bosphorus and the variety of plants grown in them. Vegetables were planted among the flowering plants in the borders, and vines, roses and other climbers were trained on walls, fences and trellises. Parterres, edged by clipped box-hedges, were filled with lemon and orange trees as well as standard pomegranate, bay and lilac bushes. Lilies, irises, sunflowers, larkspurs, mignonette, lupins, convolvulus and sweet peas were some of the flowers planted round the bushes, and flowerpots full of geraniums, carnations, lychnis, stocks, anemones, fuchsias and heliotrope stood on the terrace steps and walls. The secluded areas on the hillside were shaded by trees such as chestnut, ilex, fig, walnut, pine and cedar. The walks of the terraces were sheltered by the vine trellises and each parterre would have a central pool or a fountain. Most private gardens, like the palace and public gardens, had at least one kiosk, either situated in a tiled courtyard, or at the water's edge, or placed high up amongst the shade of trees to afford the best views. These pavilions had flat or domed roofs and the walls would be constructed with open spaces or grilles to take advantage of cool breezes, with a pool and fountain let into the tiled floor. Some kiosks would have an inner room with latticed walls for entertaining while others would simply be a shelter from the sun open at the front and with a door or

1 Evliya Çelebi, *Narrative of Travels*, translated by J. Von Hammer (London, 1834).

2 C. White, *Three Years in Constantinople*, 3 vols, (London, 1844).

window at the back for through breezes [*see* 4]. Garden kiosks of various periods and designs can be seen today in palace gardens such as the Topkapi Saraye or the Yildiz Palace in Istanbul. There was Persian influence in kiosks built by Mehmed II in the 15th century and, in turn, small Ottoman-designed pavilions became a feature of gardens in Egypt during the Ottoman rule there.

Tools and equipment used by gardeners were simple and changed very little over the centuries. Baskets carried on asses or on the backs of gardeners were a substitute for wheelbarrows. A century before White described the tools used by gardeners, Evliya Çelebi mentions those carried in one of the Processions of the Guilds in Istanbul as hoes, spades, rakes and pruning or grafting knives.

Shortly after his conquest of Istanbul in 1453, Mehmed II laid out a garden on what is now the site of the Dolmabahçe Palace. In the 17th century Ahmed I and his son, Osman II, extended the garden by filling in the small harbour there. All ships using Istanbul were ordered to load up with stones and to drop them into the sea at that point. 'Dolmabahçe' literally means 'filled-in garden'.

Creation and upkeep of gardens was carried out by successive Ottoman sultans and, to a lesser degree, by their courtiers and palace officials. Hundreds of gardeners, including specialist grafters, were employed and plants were ordered from far and wide. It is recorded that plants were brought to the palace gardens from throughout Turkey, particularly bulbs from Anatolia and thousands of trees of all kinds from Izmet. Bulbs were also imported from outside Turkey for there is a record of half a million hyacinth bulbs having been ordered from Aleppo in 1595. Works were written on flowers in general and also on single species such as tulips and hyacinths. Textiles, Iznik pottery, architecture, tiles, bookbindings and miniatures featured flowers from the early 16th century, while the language is full of the imagery of the garden paradise. Exquisite designs incorporating flowers and trees cut out of paper and formed into tiny collages are an Ottoman speciality which reached its peak in the late 18th century [*see* 2].

The obsession with tulips culminated in the so-called Tulip Era (*Lala Devre*) of the early 18th century when 'tulipomania' led to economic ruin and the deposition of the sultan, Ahmed III, in 1730. His reign became notorious for the fanatical love of gardens and flowers, particularly tulips, which eventually led to his downfall. The craze was shared by his son-in-law and Grand Vizier, Ibrahim Paşa, and, to a lesser degree, by his courtiers and nobles who vied with each other in the acquisition of rare tulip bulbs and in the splendour of their gardens. Bulbs were used by officials as a means to obtain favours from the Sultan, including high rank. Aided and abetted by Ibrahim Paşa, Ahmed III spent a fortune on buying rare varieties and creating tulip gardens in the grounds of his various palaces.

Besides his passion for tulips, Ahmed III was a lover of all flowers and gardens; he not only created gardens but decorated the interiors of his new buildings in the Topkapi Saraye complex with flowers. The dining room in the Fourth Court is known as the Orchard Room from its wallpaintings of flowers and bowls of fruit, and the ceiling of the Library, built in 1719 in the Third Court, is decorated with paintings of flowers. He laid out a tulip garden in the Fourth Court [3], the part of the Topkapi Saraye grounds furthest from the main entrance. It leads up from the building now used as the restaurant, to a terrace with fountains and a pool.

3 An album photograph of the former tulip garden established by Ahmed III in the Fourth Court of the Topkapi Saraye. One of a series of photographs commissioned c.1880 by Abdul Hamid II. [Album 4 (10)]

4 Entertainment in a garden
pavilion, sheltered from the
sun, c.1580. [Or. 7084, f. 1a]

Beyond the terrace is the Circumcision Room with ceramic tiles bearing designs that include flowers growing in the garden – tulips, carnations, prunus and others [see 6]. The Tulip Garden was the setting for the Tulip Festival held by Ahmed III at the time of the full moon each April. The gardens were decorated with cages of singing birds and coloured lights. Vases of flowers interspersed with lamps were put on shelves made for the purpose and other small lamps were fastened to the shells of the tortoises that trundled about the flower beds and paths. When the ladies of the Harem visited the gardens, all men, except the eunuch guards, were banished. A gate leads out of these gardens to the road that slopes down to the Gülhâne Park, once the outer garden of the Fifth Court of the Topkapi Saraye, but now a public park. A week-long Tulip Festival is held every year in Gülhâne Park at the beginning of April when the beds of tulips are at their best.

Ahmed III created other gardens round his palace at the lower end of the Golden Horn on the shore opposite Eyup. He built a series of kiosks in the meadows at Kağithâne where two streams flow into the Golden Horn. Known as the Sweet Waters of Europe [5], it became polluted by industrialization. Now, however, steps are being taken to clean up the environment and to restore the pavilions. In its heyday people flocked

5 A late 19th-century view of the Sweet Waters of Europe (Kağithâne) [see also 1]. [Album 6, (26)]

6 Ceramic tiles in the Topkapi Saraye bearing a variety of flower designs, photograph c.1880. [Album 7 (37)]

7 Houses and gardens along the Bosphorus, 1738–39. [Or. 13882, ff. 68b–69a).

there on foot, by oxcart or by boat and were entertained by buskers, musicians, acrobats and fortune-tellers, and the vendors of fruit, sweets and nuts who hawked their wares [*see* 1]. A similar valley near the Anadolu Hisar on the Bosphorus was known as the Sweet Waters of Asia, a notable feature there being a handsome fountain.

It was during the reign of Ahmed III that the courtiers and wealthy of Istanbul, following his example, built their mansions and wooden *yalis* at the water's edge down the Bosphorus, with tulip gardens laid out behind them [7, 8]. Archival material in the Topkapi Saraye Museum in Istanbul gives details of bulbs imported from Europe and also of an Act of 1727–28 which increased the amount of tax payable on tulip bulbs. Manuscripts of the 18th and 19th centuries list the names and descriptions of many tulips which are mainly of the highly-prized lily species with sharp-pointed petals. The ideal tulip, which was almond-shaped with petal points as sharp as needles, is the variety that appears on textiles and

tiles. Tulips given exotic names such as Petals of Love or Rose Arrow, were of every colour or combination of colours known at the time. Although the excesses of this period led to the downfall of Ahmed III there was no lessening in the popularity of tulips which remain a favourite flower, still grown in quantities in public and private gardens. Ogier Ghiselin de Busbecq, the Habsburg Ambassador to Turkey from 1554–62, during the reign of Sultan Suleyman I (the Magnificent) is usually credited with taking tulips back to Vienna and thus introducing them into Europe.[3]

Tulips featured in textile and Iznik pottery designs from the early 16th century and also in Ottoman book illustrations or miniatures. A miniature of *circa* 1520 [9] of a young prince on his way to visit his beloved, portrays him as carrying a bouquet of tulips to present to her. There are no tulips represented amongst the wild flowers in the miniature which may imply that even as early as this, they were particularly special and highly prized.

8 A late 19th-century album photograph of houses and gardens along the Bosphorus. [Album 4 (2)]

9 Designs in textiles, Iznik pottery and book illustrations from the early 16th century onwards reveal the Ottoman love of tulips; in this miniature (c.1520) a young prince prepares to present a bouquet of tulips to his beloved. [Or. 13948, f. 101b]

3 E. S. Forster, *The Turkish Letters of Ogier Ghiselin de Busbecq, Imperial Ambassador at Constantinople, 1554–62*, translated by E. S. Forster (Oxford, 1927).

*10 The garden of the Military
School of Medicine, Istanbul,
c.1886. [Album 15 (23)]*

Illustrated records and contemporary accounts of festivals and processions held by the sultans during celebrations are also witness to the importance of gardens and to the enormous number of men employed in horticulture. Amongst the floats in a procession during a festival held by Suleyman the Magnificent in 1530 were those of miniature gardens complete with orchards, pavilions, beds of flowers and pools. Evliya Çelebi (died 1679, *see* note 1), during his travels in Europe and Asia, was in Istanbul in 1638 when Murad IV reviewed the Guilds which passed in procession before him at the Alay Kiosk (Procession Pavilion) with emblems of their respective trades. Çelebi relates that the guilds numbered a thousand and one and goes on to describe their floats, portable workshops, studios, shops, equipment and tools. They passed in front of the Sultan and his entourage demonstrating the skills of every imaginable trade. The gardeners formed a body of men carrying hoes, spades, saws and all the implements of gardening. Watering machines were drawn by oxen, and the gardeners, who wore floral creations on their heads, tossed flowers to the spectators. The Guild of Grafters, some 500 strong, carried plates of fruit on their heads and branches in their hands together with knives, saws and other grafting tools. They were reputedly skilled in grafting vines and mulberries to obtain new varieties.

Palaces on the Bosphorus with formal gardens included Dolmabahçe,

built 1843–56, and Beylerbeyi Palace situated near the Bosphorus Bridge, built in 1861–65. When Abdul Hamid II succeeded in 1876, he preferred to live in the Yildiz Palace high up overlooking the Bosphorus. There he created ten acres of rambling gardens and parkland which contained several buildings including a small palace, as well as several pavilions, arbours and ponds, in addition to flower borders, shrubs and trees. He had a miniature canal constructed with small landing stages equivalent to those situated at villages up and down the Bosphorus. These gardens, which have been restored, demonstrate the difference between Ottoman Turkish gardens and those of Iran and India, with the emphasis on winding paths, fountains and pools. Small pavilions at the water's edge echo the *yalis* on the shore of the Bosphorus.

Abdul Hamid II had a series of photographs taken for the Yildiz Palace library to provide a record of every aspect of life in Istanbul and elsewhere in Turkey. He was anxious that his country's achievements should be more widely known and recognised. With that end in view, he sent handsomely-bound volumes of a large selection of photographs to the Library of Congress in Washington in 1893 and a further 51 albums to the British Museum in London in 1894 and 1895.[4] Mostly dating from the 1880s, these albums include photographs of palaces, academies and schools with their respective gardens [10, 11] and views of the Golden

11 The garden of the Imperial Ottoman School, Istanbul, c.1880. [Album 47, (3)]

4 Carney E. S. Gavin and the Harvard Semitic Museum (eds), 'Imperial Self-Portrait: the Ottoman Empire as revealed in the Sultan Abdul Hamid II's photographic albums. A pictorial selection with catalogue, concordance, indices and brief essays', *Journal of Turkish Studies* (Turkluk Bilgisi Arastirmalari), vol. 12 (Harvard, 1988).

Horn and the Bosphorus. Among several photographs of the Yildiz Palace gardens is one of a small boat on a stretch of water [12], possibly a miniature boat for the canal. A late 16th-century Ottoman miniature [13], one of several illustrations to a collection of fables and stories, is of a king, some 300 years earlier, sailing a small boat on a garden pool.

The Turkish people's love of flowers and gardens is as much in evidence today as it ever was. The tulip festivals in the parks and gardens are occasions for great rejoicing and enjoyment by the crowds who flock to them in April, and flower markets do a roaring trade. Gardens surrounding tombs and graves in cemeteries such as those in Eyup and Bursa are carefully tended as are those of the mosques and museums. Museum gardens in Istanbul range from the extensive grounds of the Topkapi Saraye Museum to the delightful fig orchards of the Museum of Mosaics and to the tiny courtyard with its pool and fountain enclosed in baytrees and box hedges at the old Museum of Turkish and Islamic Art near the Suleymaniye Mosque.

12 The Yildiz Palace garden, Istanbul, c.1880. [Album 7 (20)]

13 *Garden entertainments: in an illustration to a late 16th-century manuscript, a king sails a miniature boat in a garden pool.*
[*Add. 15153, f. 382a*]

چو مرا ملک رباب دیده
سلسل کرد دلش شاه دیده

14 A walled garden, from a
illustration to a collection o
poems, c.1396 [see 16]

15 A 16th-century miniatu
depicting Timur in the
Garden of Heart's Delight,
Samarkand.
[IOL MS 137, f. 254b]

Iran

The love of flowers and interest in gardens have been features of life in Iran down the centuries. Archaeological surveys have produced plans for palaces with extensive gardens dating back to the pre-Islamic Sassanian dynasty (AD 224–641). In addition, travellers to Iran from that period right down to the present day give descriptions of gardens in their diaries and journals. Several accounts, particularly from the early 15th century

onwards, were recorded in diaries kept by envoys sent on diplomatic missions to the courts of Iran, and included descriptions of the royal gardens where they would be received and entertained on a lavish scale. Only the ruins of such grand gardens, which delighted and surprised those early travellers, still exist, but present-day visitors to Iran who are given hospitality in private homes know how the smallest garden or courtyard can provide coolness and shade as relief from the searing heat and arid landscape. To go through a door in a high wall off a dusty road or off one of the teeming noisy alleyways of a bazaar, is to enter another world of peace, coolness and tranquillity.

Whether on a grand scale or in the simplest garden, the layout usually consists of a central pool with a fountain and four channels at right angles to each other enclosing flower beds, while shrubs, shady trees and fruit trees line the paths to provide essential shade. This scheme, known as the *chahar bagh* (literally 'four gardens'), has been used in large or small gardens in Iran for centuries and was introduced to India by the first Mughal emperor, Babur, after 1526. Gardens retained the original plan under successive Mughal emperors but with increasing emphasis on the use of water. Narrow channels developed into terraced canals with waterfalls, chutes and series of fountains providing a remarkable vista.

The *chahar bagh* was the ideal garden, the earthly paradise, providing coolness and shade to offset the heat of an Iranian summer in which six to ten inches of rainfall is the annual average over much of the country, apart from the semi-tropical Caspian region. In a country with such low rainfall, plants of any kind could not be grown without irrigation and a regular supply of water has been provided for centuries by the remarkable *qanat* system which dates back to about the sixth century BC. Water tables form at the base of mountains from the melting snow which seeps through the porous sandstone and gravel and a tunnel on different levels is constructed to divert the water to where it is needed. Additional shafts are constructed, at intervals of fifty yards or so, from the tunnel to the surface to provide exit holes and these are used to dispose of soil being dug out and to provide air ducts and inspection pits. From the air these holes resemble a series of small bomb craters strung across the desert. The work is very highly skilled and the *qanat* men are considered to be the elite of the Iranian workforce. The water supply, which is strictly controlled, is available all the year round and is used for the irrigation of crops, orchards and gardens.

From the 14th century gardens have been a feature of Persian* miniatures and are often the setting or background of incidents related in romantic epic poems and tales, whilst the language of Iran (Farsi) is full of the imagery of flowers and of Paradise in the guise of a garden. These

*The word 'Persian', so long used in the context of the miniature painting of Iran, has been retained in this chapter to avoid confusion with pre-Islamic Iranian art.

miniatures are a valuable source of information concerning the layout of gardens and of the details of water courses, various kinds of pavilions and summer houses and of plants and trees included in them. In contrast to Ottoman Turkish gardens with their rambling paths and somewhat haphazard layout, Persian gardens were geometric in design. The cross channels ran at right angles to the central reservoir or pool which might be round, square or rectangular, hexagonal or octagonal, with scalloped or shamrock edges, often with a central fountain. In larger gardens, further channels would cross the central one at right angles forming several *chahar baghs* in one garden. This scheme or plan is very clearly demonstrated in the designs of the so-called garden carpets, which include fish in the channels, ducks in the pools, flower beds between the channels and shrubs and fruit trees in the outlying ground, the whole pattern enclosed in avenues of shady trees.

The concept of the Persian garden, like other Iranian traditions, was adopted by the ruling descendants of the Mongols who had swept over Iran in the 13th century. Gardens are mentioned by Marco Polo who spent nine months at Tabriz in north-west Iran in the late 13th century. Just over a hundred years later, Clavijo,[1] the Spanish envoy sent by Henry III of Castile, gave detailed descriptions of his arrival at Samarkand in 1404 and the events that took place.

Timur (Tamerlane), who died in 1405, made Samarkand his capital and created several gardens there. These gardens and life at the court of Timur were vividly described by Clavijo. He writes of a walled garden full of fruit trees and adjacent to a vineyard, also enclosed by a wall, which had a central stream with water channels flowing amongst the trees. The Garden of Heart's Delight (*Dilkusha*), [15] where Timur first received Clavijo and which contained many trees, had been constructed in 1397 in the meadows outside Samarkand, known as Kani Gil, where Timur periodically used to hold celebrations for immense gatherings of his people. Other gardens created at Samarkand by Timur and his successors included the Garden of the Plane Trees, the New Garden, the Paradise Garden and the Northern Garden. Altogether some 15 or 16 Samarkand gardens are mentioned in contemporary accounts of the 15th century. They were also visited by Babur as a young man and described in his memoirs, and his own abiding interest in gardens may well have been inspired by them.

Clavijo also writes of tents, awnings and palaces located in the gardens. The awnings were described as being long and high, secured above by cords attached to two poles so that they provided shade without excluding cooling breezes. These awnings were a regular feature of gardens for centuries and are illustrated in late 15th-century, mid 16th-century, and later miniatures [*see* 19, 20].

1 Ruy Gonzalez de Clavijo, *Clavijo, Embassy is Tamelane, 1403–1406*, translated by Guy le Strange (London, 1928).

Permanent garden pavilions, constructed in various styles, ranged from the simplest which provided a roof for shade, to a small palace with inner rooms, and these pavilions took the place of the tents of the earlier gardens. The small simple pavilions, the equivalent of permanent awnings, were open on three sides to allow cool air to circulate, while the larger buildings were constructed on two floors with balconies and inner rooms for receptions, recreation and entertainment and, light and airy with open views, were an extension of the garden. Contemporary miniatures portray these pavilions as places for entertainment of all kinds, music, feasting, painting, discussions and hospitality. The simplest designs included plain tiled floors but the grander the pavilion the more ambitious were the methods of cooling the building by incorporating pools, fountains and cross-channels.

A miniature illustrating a collection of poems dated 1396, and contemporary with the reign of Timur, is probably a true likeness of the kind of walled garden and small palace described by Clavijo and associated with Timur [14, 16]. It shows a garden house or small palace set in a walled garden in which the stream outside the wall in the foreground has been diverted to flow within the garden. Red waterlilies grow in the water and violets and pollarded willows line its banks. Daylilies and hollyhocks are growing in the garden as well as in the arid ground outside the walls while fruit trees, poplars and plane trees provide shade.

Over the centuries, wherever the centre of power was in Iran, whether Samarkand, Herat, Tabriz, Qazvin, Isfahan, Shiraz or Tehran, palaces, houses and pavilions were constructed with their accompanying gardens. They were built by the rulers themselves or by governors of provinces, courtiers and high officials. Herat, now in Afghanistan, was an important centre for hundreds of years. Timur's son, Shahrukh (died 1447), made Herat his capital, laying out new gardens and renovating existing ones. These gardens were designed on the *chahar bagh* geometric plan with the usual waterchannels, pools, flowerbeds, orchards, pavilions and avenues of shady trees, all surrounded by a wall. The ruler, Sultan Husayn Bayqara, a noted patron of the arts, was crowned in 1468 in the Garden of the Ravens and early in his reign ordered the construction of a *chahar bagh* which eventually covered a hundred acres outside the city. It is on record that the scribes and artists who copied and illustrated books for Sultan Husayn's extensive library worked in pavilions or under awnings in the White Garden at Herat. One of the fine manuscripts copied and illustrated for Sultan Husayn in 1494 includes a miniature of the interior of a garden pavilion [17]. A window at the back, providing a cross-draught, opens out onto the garden with its flowering and fruit trees, and vases of flowers are placed on the tiled floor either side of the pool. Water flows across the floor by way of a channel running from the central octagonal

16 The stream in the foreground of this illustration, with red water lilies, violets and pollarded willows along its banks, has been diverted to flow inside the walled garden. [Add. 18113, 18b]

17 The interior of a garden pavilion, from a manuscript dated 1494. A cooling water channel flows through the building to a central pool, and flowering and fruit trees are visible through the doorway to the garden behind. [Or. 6810, 62b]

pool. Another contemporary double-page miniature dating from the same period illustrates the kind of elaborate entertainment that took place in Persian gardens in the cool of the evening [see 19]. While waiting for the banquet to be prepared, the young prince, seated on a low throne under a superb awning, is being entertained by musicians. The peculiar angle of the awning is explained by the fact that Persian artists ignored perspective. Shadows, too, are non-existent, regardless of whether the scene takes place in brilliant sunshine or by moonlight.

Besides the gardens at Samarkand, the future Mughal emperor Babur was very impressed by those he saw in Herat in 1506 when he was in his early twenties.[2] Babur's interest in plants and gardens is evident from his memoirs, for he constantly wrote of gardens he had laid out or altered and of plants he had grown, whether in Kabul or, after 1526, when he was in India. Of the gardens he saw in Herat, he mentions several by name including the Garden of the Ravens and the White Garden. Others were the Town Garden and the Garden of Heart's Delight.

Tabriz in north-west Iran was an important centre for centuries and like Isfahan, Herat and other cities had famous gardens. Marco Polo wrote of the splendid gardens he saw during the months he spent there in 1300. At the end of the 15th century a magnificent garden known as the Eight Paradises (*Hasht Bihisht*) was constructed by the then Turkman rulers. In the 16th century when Shah Tahmasp made the city his capital, it became a famous centre of book production under his patronage. Two miniatures from a manuscript of the Five Poems (or *Khamsa*) of Nizami, which was copied and illustrated for Shah Tahmasp at Tabriz between 1539 and 1543, illustrate the coolness and tranquillity of Persian gardens. In one the small permanent pavilion is a simple structure of a roof supported by four poles, providing shade but still open to breezes [18]. A fountain is playing in the larger of the two pools set in the tiled floor with a channel of water running through both pools. A gate in the railings surrounding the courtyard opens out into the garden near a stream which meanders between banks of flowers and small rose bushes. Shade is provided by prunus, poplar, cypress and oriental plane (*chenar*) trees, and irises, poppies and hollyhocks grow in the bare ground beyond the garden.

The story which this scene illustrates centres round a rose, one of many poems and tales in Persian literature concerned with flowers. Two rival physicians quarrelled about the efficacy of poisons and eventually agreed to put their theories to the test. The wiser of the two swallowed an antidote with the deadly pill given to him by his rival. He then picked a spray of roses and breathed a spell on it, before handing it to his opponent who, greatly fearing the power of the spell, smelled the roses and fell dead from terror. The artist of this miniature has painted the roses lying on the tiles with particular care.

2 A. S. Beveridge (translator), *The Babur-nāma in English* (repr. London, 1969).

Flowers most often included in miniatures are roses, peonies, narcissus, pomegranate, prunus, irises of various colours, hollyhocks and daylilies. Strangely, crown imperials do not occur in Persian illustrations, although they appear regularly in Indian Mughal art. Sir John Chardin, when describing flowers he saw in Iran during his travels in the 17th century,[3] includes a rose bush of which he writes: '[it] bore upon one and the same branch, Roses of three Colours, some Yellow, others Yellow and White, and others Yellow and Red'. An illustration in the Houghton *Shahnama* (Book of Kings), a manuscript now dispersed, which is contemporary with The British Library's *Khamsa* of Nizami (*i.e.* mid-16th century), includes this particular rose. Illustrations by the most famous artists of the day for their royal patrons portray details of gardens with great care, including the layout, pavilions and plants and trees. This is also true of other aspects of contemporary life at court including costumes, weapons, furniture and

18 This miniature from the story of two physicians and a rose, 1539–43, illustrates some characteristic, cooling features of Persian gardens: a permanent pavilion, with pools and water channels set in a tiled floor.
[Or. 2265, f. 26b]

3 Sir John Chardin, *Travels in Persia*, with an introduction by Sir Percy Sykes (London, 1927).

19 Elaborate entertainments in a garden, 1493. A young prince shelters under a superb awning, while a banquet is being prepared. [Add. 25900, ff. 3b–4a]

20 A garden scene depicting gardeners at work, a central pool with fountain and channel and an awning providing protection from the sun, from a manuscript dated 1539–43. [Or. 2265, f. 48b]

musical instruments, making these miniatures an important source of historical information.

The second painting, also from Shah Tahmasp's *Khamsa* of Nizami includes an awning attached to two poles by cords and is similar to those described by Clavijo earlier [20]. Lack of perspective again shows the awning pitched at a peculiar angle. The small courtyard in this painting has one large central round pool with a fountain and channel. The stream flowing off the mountains in the background has been diverted round the garden to emerge in the foreground, flanked by willows, dark irises and hollyhocks. The water, originally painted silver, has been blackened by oxydization.

Shiraz, an oasis town in the south of Iran, has been famous for its
gardens for centuries. Entering Shiraz by the desert road leading from
Persepolis, the whole city appears to be one large garden, with an
abundance of cypress, plane and fruit trees. Royal gardens created in the
19th century still exist and others surround the tombs of the famous poets
Sa'di and Hafiz. The Garden of Heart's Delight (every city has one of that
name) in Shiraz is very beautiful, with long flower beds full of roses and
lilies, flanked by cypress, orange and pomegranate trees and bushes with
a central channel and pool. Private gardens in Shiraz, as elsewhere, are
cherished. One example is the small Pars Museum, an octagonal building,
once a private house, set in a mulberry plantation and surrounded by its
own garden. Both the setting and the garden are exquisite and on a par
with the tiny courtyard with its fountains, flowers and baytrees at the old
Museum of Turkish and Islamic Art near the Suleymaniye Mosque in
Istanbul. It is well worth seeking out these small gardens for they retain
the old traditions of garden layout and are quite delightful.

Shiraz, as elsewhere, was a centre of book production for hundreds of
years. The academies were never on the grand scale of Tabriz or Isfahan,
but their work was always interesting. An early 16th-century illustration
(c.1505) includes a simple garden as a background. A young man
returning home from his travels could hear women laughing and talking
in his garden as he approached his home and discovered them bathing in
his walled garden [21]. This charmingly naive illustration includes a
stream flowing through a conduit under the wall into the pool. The young
man, anxious about the identity of the intruders, but not wishing to be
seen, is peering, upside-down, through the gap in the wall. Another
unusual detail in a late 16th-century manuscript [22] is the carefully drawn
vine, heavy with bunches of grapes, winding its way up a plane tree to
burst out at the top of the page.

Sir Thomas Herbert[4] who travelled in Iran between 1627 and 1629
visited Shiraz and wrote that 'the gardens are many, and both large and
beautiful. Most are enclosed in walls fourteen feet high and four feet
thick'. Besides listing fruit trees, he noted that the gardens 'are spacious
with plenty of trees, abound in cypresses, chenars, elm, ash, pines, oaks,
myrtles and maples' and that ropes were attached to tree branches as
swings. There were 'flowers rare to the eye, sweet to the smell and useful
in physic'.

Herbert also spent some time in Isfahan and wrote that 'gardens here
for grandeur and fragrance are such as no city in Asia outvies'. This was
during the reign of Shah 'Abbas I (died 1629) who was the greatest
creator of gardens in Iran, equal to the Mughal emperors in India. Shah
'Abbas had been brought up in Herat and no doubt gardens there
influenced him, as they had Babur a century earlier. Shah 'Abbas moved

4 Thomas Herbert, *Travels in
Persia, 1627–1629* (London, 1928).

his capital from Qazvin further south to Isfahan in 1598 where he set about creating splendid gardens. Previously Isfahan had been a simple oasis town which he had visited from time to time and no doubt he recognized its location as being favourable. Situated on a fertile plain below the Zagros mountains, in an otherwise arid desert, it was ideal for creating gardens. Most Iranian cities grew up near mountains so that the qanat system of water supply could be developed but Isfahan had the additional advantage of the Zayanda River that runs through the plain. The only part of the gardens laid out by Shah 'Abbas I in existence today is the Chahar Bagh, originally built as a promenade, but now a busy thoroughfare through Isfahan. It was constructed in the early 17th century as a promenade stretching some two miles to the gardens, Hazar Jarib (Thousand Acres), beyond the river, from the royal palace and gardens, Naqsh-i Jahan. A wide water channel with fountains and pools at intervals ran down its entire length, with smaller channels on either side. Pavilions and summer houses were built in the gardens each side of the promenade, including the Garden of the Nightingales, the Garden of the Vineyard and the Mulberry Garden. None of these original buildings constructed by Shah 'Abbas have survived. The mud walls were susceptible to extremes of climate and Sir John Chardin, who was in Isfahan in the late 17th century, vividly describes a destructive storm in which the mud walls were dissolved: '23rd December fell another Rain accompanied with such furious Storms that I never saw the like. It lasted four and twenty Hours and filled with Water not only the Streets, but also the Houses and Gardens'. The river overflowed and the Chahar Bagh was under four feet of water. 'The Gardens thereabouts were laid under Water and the Houses of Pleasure overthrown.'

Sir Thomas Herbert describes the Hazar Jarib gardens as having a series of terraces which led up to a large central 12-sided reservoir with fountains. Three gates led through the walls into the garden, the northern gate having a pavilion of six rooms, in which the ground floor had marble pools. Herbert mentions that water was brought 'by extra-ordinary charge and toil from the Elburz', probably by the qanat system. Ornate pavilions and small palaces were built in the gardens. At the opposite end of the Chahar Bagh was the palace and gardens, Naqsh-i Jahan, also laid out by Shah 'Abbas and much used by him. Iskandar Beg Munshi[5] describes the New Year (Nuruz) celebrations held by Shah 'Abbas each March when he was in Isfahan. These usually took place in the Naqsh-i Jahan gardens. The Iranian New Year has always been celebrated out-of-doors and Shah 'Abbas held royal garden parties, to which he invited vast numbers of his subjects. Each group of merchants, officials and ordinary citizens had their allotted spaces along the banks of the stream while courtiers, viziers and other officers of state were

5 Eskander Beg Monshi, History of Shah 'Abbas the Great, translated by R. M. Savory, Persian Heritage Series 28, 2 vols, (Boulder, Colorado, 1978).

21 A simple walled garden
with bathing pool and stream,
c.1505.
[IOL MS 387, f. 279a]

22 A magnificent vine in a
late 16th-century manuscript
illustration.
[Add. 27257, f. 44b]

allocated places by the huge pool 'as big as a small lake'. Extra pavilions of various designs were decorated with lights, and silk brocade canopies and gold tents were erected. Shah 'Abbas himself would go amongst his guests who were entertained with feasting and music.

Other gardens constructed by Shah 'Abbas were described by Herbert and Iskandar Beg Munshi. One, mentioned by Herbert, was situated in the desert outside Isfahan and he describes it as full of fruit trees and flowers, naming peaches, apricots, pomegranates, plums, cherries, apples, pears, chestnuts, damask roses, tulips and other flowers. It had streams, artificial grottoes, stone pools lined with marble and a summer-house of 12 rooms. Herbert also mentions that gardens in the former capital, Qazvin, are many and large but not to be compared with those in Isfahan and Shiraz. Qazvin was irrigated by the *qanat* system and was notable for the abundant fruit grown there including most of those named above as well as grapes, figs, water and musk melons, citrus fruits and various nuts including hazels, filberts, walnuts, almonds and pistachios.

Shah 'Abbas I conquered the region of Mazandaran near the Caspian Sea in 1596–97 and this area held as much delight for him as did Kashmir for the Mughal emperors Jahangir and Shahjahan. In a country of extremes of temperature, the fertile Caspian region is distinguished by a semi-tropical climate with a relatively high annual rainfall of 40–60 inches, some five times the average for the country. Deciduous forests, rice, tea, cotton, sugar-cane, tobacco and citrus fruits are included among crops in an area where adequate irrigation is not a problem. Shah 'Abbas made a highway through Mazandaran, with caravanserais (fortified overnight stopping points) *en route*, leading to the Caspian. At Ashraf (modern Behshahr), about five miles from the Caspian Sea, he built a palace and laid out parks and gardens, the remains of which can still be seen. He also built houses and palaces along the coast at Amol, Sari and Barfarush. Sir John Chardin was in Mazandaran one February in the 1670s 'at which time I was in a manner charm'd and inchanted [*sic*] with it; for the whole Country is nothing but one continued Garden, or a perfect kind of Paradise, as the Persians call it. The Causeways and Highways appear like so many Alleys of Orange-Trees, bordered on either side with fine Parterrees [*sic*], and flowery Garden'.

Shah 'Abbas I died in 1629 aged 60 and was succeeded first by Shah Safi' and then by Shah 'Abbas II (died 1666). The Chihil Sutun, a large garden pavilion, was built by 'Abbas II in 1647 and survives, with its garden, much as it was when first built. Just off the Chahar Bagh in Isfahan, it was used by 'Abbas II for receptions and entertaining. One of the grander garden pavilions, it resembles a small palace with open sides, water channels, marble pools and tiled floors. Airy, yet protected

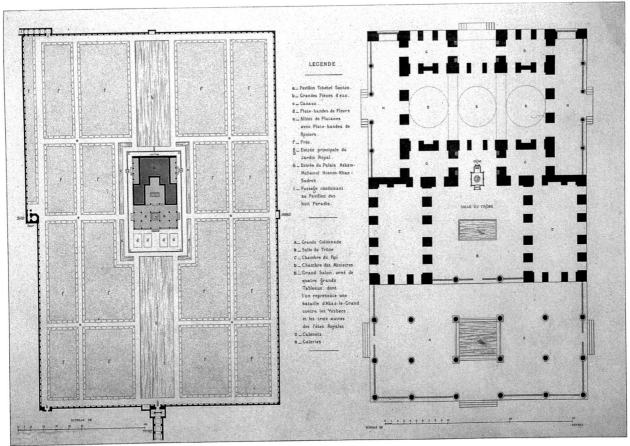

LEGENDE

a _ Pavillon Tchehel Souton.
b _ Grandes Pièces d'eau.
c _ Canaux.
d _ Plate-bandes de Fleurs
e _ Allées de Platanes
avec Plate-bandes de
Rosiers.
f _ Prés.
g _ Entrée principale du
Jardin Royal.
h _ Entrée du Palais Asham-
Mahamel Hussen-Khan-
Sadreh.
i _ Passage conduisant
au Pavillon des
huit Paradis.

A _ Grande Colonnade
B _ Salle du Trône
C _ Chambre du Roi
D _ Chambre des Ministres
E _ Grand Salon orné de
quatre grands
Tableaux, dont
l'un représente une
bataille d'Abas-le-Grand
contre les Yusbecs,
et les trois autres
des fêtes Royales.
G _ Cabinets.
H _ Galeries.

from the fierce heat of the sun, with extensive views over the surrounding flower beds, it is an extension of the garden itself. The largest room, decorated with paintings, was used for receptions and there are two smaller rooms opening out on the garden. Twenty wooden pillars surrounding the large rectangular pool support the roof of the porch and the reflection of the pillars in the water is said to have inspired the name of the pavilion, Chihil Sutun or Forty Pillars. The plan published by Pascal Coste[6] in 1867 shows the pavilion situated in a garden much as it must have been in the 17th century [23]. Plane trees underplanted with rose bushes provided shade for the paths while the pavilion itself was surrounded by beds of flowers and shrubs divided by water channels in the usual *chahar bagh* plan.

The only surviving building along the Chahar Bagh, the Isfahan thoroughfare, is the Hasht Bihisht (Eight Paradises) pavilion. Situated near the Chihil Sutun, it was built during the reign of Shah Sulayman I (died 1694) in 1669 in what had been the Garden of the Nightingales in the time of Shah 'Abbas I. It is still an exquisite building but in its heyday, set in its own garden, it must have been particularly beautiful. Today it is situated, without its garden, on what has become a very busy road.

23 A 19th-century plan of Chihil Sutun, a grand garden pavilion constructed in 1647. [N Tab 2000/2, Pl. XLI]

6 Pascal Coste, *Monuments modernes de la Perse, Mesures, dessines et decrits* (Paris, 1867).

24 An illustration of love-lies-bleeding from a 19th-century manuscript of the poem, 'The secret language of sweet-scented flowers'. [Add. 22789, f. 324b]

Another extensive garden laid out in 17th-century Isfahan was called the Sa'atabad (Abode of Felicity) which was situated on the south bank of the river. Coste published several engravings of its palaces and pavilions in the 19th century before they were all destroyed. Another record of the Sa'atabad Garden is a poem 'The Secret Language of Sweet-scented Flowers' by Ramzi (*i.e.* Mirza Hadi). In his introduction, Ramzi relates how he had been summoned to the presence of Shah 'Abbas II in the garden and told to write a poem in praise of it. A manuscript of this poem in The British Library was copied and illustrated in 1835 and contains 29 paintings of flowers described in the poems. These include narcissus, violets, willow, hyacinths, irises, centaurea, larkspurs, tuberose, irises, tulips, poppies, the blossom of various fruit trees, lilies, Judas tree, white jasmine, Marvel of Peru, sweet basil, love-lies-bleeding [24] and several varieties of roses of different colours.

Besides being used as illustrations in manuscripts, flowers were painted on the borders of pages, book-bindings [25], page decorations

25 Rich floral illustrations on
a sumptuous early 19th-
century bookbinding.
[IOL Pers. MS 3558]

26 A detailed study of violets from a 16th-century manuscript page decoration. [Or. 2265, f. 396]

[26], pen-boxes and mirror-cases, particularly in the 19th century during the Qajar dynasty. Some five hundred years earlier (1396) the artist of the walled garden [*see* 21] had provided an interesting study of specific flowers as the background to a celebration in a garden [27]. From the waterlilies growing in the stream in the foreground to the roses being gathered at the top of the page, the whole scene is full of flowers. They include daylilies, violets, hollyhocks, small rose bushes, willows, white lilies and narcissus with peonies, prunus, peach, pomegranate, cypress and other trees flanking the large rosebush. Courtyards of the simplest gardens and schools would often have a large shady poplar or plane tree and careful studies of single trees are sometimes included in illustrations dating back to the 14th or 15th century [28].

Tehran, the modern capital of Iran situated below the Elburz mountains, has many gardens particularly in the suburbs such as Gulhak, Tajrish, Shimran and Niavaran. Embassies, large houses and former palaces all had large gardens, some now in ruins, but, as in every city in Iran, cool, shady gardens are still hidden away behind high walls even in the smallest alleyway.

27 A host of flowers provide the background to this late
14th-century illustration of celebrations in a garden.
[Add. 18113, f. 40b]

28 A careful study of a chenar tree in a school courtyard, 1493.
[Or. 6810, f. 106b]

India

When considering the characteristic features of Indian gardens, those that spring to mind are the magnificent landscaped gardens designed on a grand scale by the Mughals at Agra, Delhi, Lucknow, Lahore, Kashmir and elsewhere. From the time of the first Mughal emperor, Babur (died 1530), who conquered India in 1526, until the decay of the empire early in the 18th century, the Mughal rulers, high officials and governors created them. But the Indian love of gardens in fact began centuries earlier. They are mentioned in Hindu epics, particularly in descriptions of temples which were built near springs and running water. Artificial water-courses, terraces and parterres were yet to come, but beautiful natural gardens of indigenous trees of the forests and river banks are described at the sites of temples and pilgrim shrines. Illustrations of such forest scenes are included in manuscripts produced for Hindu patrons who remained relatively independent of Mughal rule [see 50 and 51]. These illustrations are in Indian styles, almost untouched by Islamic and Mughal influences.

The spread of Islam extended to India from the 13th century, and the Ganges plain was dominated by Islamic rulers who, almost certainly, were the first to introduce the *chahar bagh* (four-gardens) system from Iran. In the 16th and 17th centuries this plan, reintroduced by Babur, was expanded in Mughal gardens. Early 16th-century illustrations produced at the studios of the so-called Sultanate rulers, who had introduced traditions of book production from Iran, exhibit strong Persian character-istics of style, while depicting plants, trees and flowers alien to Iran but abundant in India, such as the banyan, pipal, mango, plantain and lotus [30].

Throughout the Mughal period, following Babur's victory at Panipat in 1526, until the reign of Aurangzib (died 1707) and the decline of the Mughal empire, splendid gardens, palaces, pavilions and tombs were created. The great gardens range in date from the Rambagh at Agra, reputedly the first laid out by Babur, to that created by Fiday Khan, Aurangzib's foster-brother, at Pinjaur near Simla in the late 17th century. Originally inspired by the Persian *chahar bagh*, the garden design was geometric with a central water channel crossed at right angles by smaller channels, each section forming a flower bed. This geometric system was retained throughout the Mughal period but in succeeding years the emphasis was increasingly laid on the use of water to enhance the landscape. Each succeeding Mughal emperor designed gardens on a yet more ambitious scale, introducing wide canals, rows of fountains, water-falls, cascades and chutes, together with small palaces and pavilions each with their own system of basement pools and channels. In terraced gardens the central channel would be so arranged that the water would fall gently from level to level or else race down cascades and waterfalls,

PAGES 44–45
29 The gardens of the Taj Mahal at Agra, painted by William Daniell in 1789 and published as an aquatint in 1801. [IOL p. 396]

activating a series of fountains on the way. Parterres divided by narrower channels were laid out at right-angles to the main canal while oriental planes (*chenars*), cypresses and other shady trees lined the paths.

Thanks to the diaries, journals and chronicles left by the Mughal emperors from Babur onwards, and to the few gardens which survive in their original form in Delhi and Kashmir, the origin, designs and development of Mughal gardens are well-documented. One of Babur's abiding interests was the creation of gardens wherever he went. A true gardener throughout his life, whether travelling or on campaign, he observed the local flowers, plants and trees, making entries about them, as well as reporting on the progress of his own gardens, in the diaries he kept so assiduously.[1]

Sixth in line of descent from Timur (Tamerlane), Babur was born in Ferghana near Samarkand in 1483. He was familiar with the gardens created by his ancestor at Samarkand and also with those at Herat which had been laid out by Timur's sons and grandsons. These gardens, designed in the *chahar bagh* system, were the main influence on those he himself created, particularly at Kabul (which, like Herat, is now in Afghanistan) and later in India. He writes of nine gardens at Samarkand, including the Dilkusha (Heart's Delight) with its avenue of white poplars leading to the Turquoise Gate. During a visit to Herat in 1506, Babur mentions, amongst others, the White Garden and describes its summer house ('Joy house') as 'a sweet little abode' built in two storeys.

Babur's favourite garden was the one that he created at Kabul, known as the *Bagh-i Vafa* (Garden of Fidelity) [31]. In an entry in his diary during October 1519 he writes: 'Those were the days of the garden's beauty: its lawns were one sheet of trefoil: its pomegranate trees yellowed to autumn splendour.' He laid the garden out in 1508–09 on rising ground facing south and when he went to India he sent back plantains and sugar-cane for the garden where 'they did very well'. He describes the garden as lying high, with running water close by, and a mild winter climate. A stream flowed past a small hill in the middle of the garden, on which there were four garden plots. Round the reservoir to the south-west there were orange and pomegranate trees, the whole encircled by trefoil lawns. 'Truly that garden is admirably situated.' The late 16th-century artist depicting the garden has followed Babur's description very carefully, illustrating the plants mentioned and the water flowing into the channels that form the *chahar bagh*.

Another garden created by Babur, also near Kabul, was at Istalif, one of the villages in the fertile fruit-growing area near the Paghman mountains. Babur describes planes, holm-oaks and Judas trees as growing in abundance round a spring nearby. He had a round seat placed on the hillside, diverted a stream to flow past it and put in cuttings of planes

1 A. S. Beveridge (translator), *The Barhur-nāma in English* (repr. London, 1969).

48

30 An early 16th-century
(Indian Sultanate) garden
scene, showing the influence
of strong Persian
characteristics of style.
[Or. 4535, f. 83b]

31 The Mughal Emperor Babur's Bagh-i Vafa (Garden of Fidelity) at Kabul, illustrated in a late 16th-century chronicle of Babur's life. [Or. 3714, f. 173b]

and sycamores. In all, he created ten gardens in and around Kabul, in addition to the one he designed for his future burial ground. This tomb garden was restored and extended by his great-great-grandson, Shah-jahan (died 1666) who commented in his chronicles on the magnificence of some plane trees originally planted at Kabul by Babur.

It was the lack of rising ground, necessary to make terraces, and of natural streams for irrigation purposes that Babur found so daunting on the Indian plains, when he decided to create gardens at Agra after his conquest of India in 1526. Previous rulers had constructed canals and artificial lakes but water was generally raised from wells by the use of oxen yoked to a wheel or by a treadmill [32]. Babur used wells and invented improved methods for drawing water from them. 'One of the great defects of Hindustan being its lack of running waters, it kept coming to my mind that waters should be made to flow by means of wheels erected wherever I might settle down, also that grounds should be laid out in an orderly and symmetrical way ... then plots of garden were laid out with suitable borders and parterres in every corner and in every border, rose and narcissus in perfect arrangement.' As well as sending plants back to his gardens at Kabul, Babur imported plants into India, and a melon-grower from Balkh (then in Iran), a city renowned for melons. The lack of water channels and of gardens initially deterred Babur when he surveyed possible sites near Agra. He was so discouraged that he abandoned his original idea of making a *chahar bagh* there, only to change his mind when nothing better than the grounds 'so bad and unattractive we traversed them with a hundred disgusts and repulsions' could be found. Eventually he designed his first garden in India at Agra, reputedly the Rambagh, still there today but considerably altered.

What Babur began in India, his successors and their followers continued, and gardens, including tomb gardens, were created all over Central India and, later, in Kashmir. Wherever he went in India, Babur noted plants hitherto unfamiliar to him. He was so taken with red oleanders he saw in a garden in Gwalior, south of Agra, that he collected some for his own gardens. He listed and described trees and plants such as mango, banana ('out of its leaves rises heartlike, a bud which resembles a sheep's heart. The fruit has two pleasant qualities, one that it peels easily, the other that it has neither stone nor fibre'), mimusops, jack-fruit, monkeyjack, myrobalan, oranges of various kinds, limes [33], lemons, oleander, screwpine, hibiscus, banyan, pipal and many others.

In 1506 Babur held celebrations in the Chahar Bagh at Kabul for the birth of his first son, Humayun, and the miniature depicting this event is a good illustration of a royal Mughal garden [38]. Raised stone platforms were built under the shade of trees, covered with a carpet and given extra

32 *Oxen used to draw up water for the irrigation of flower beds.*
[*Detail from 34*]

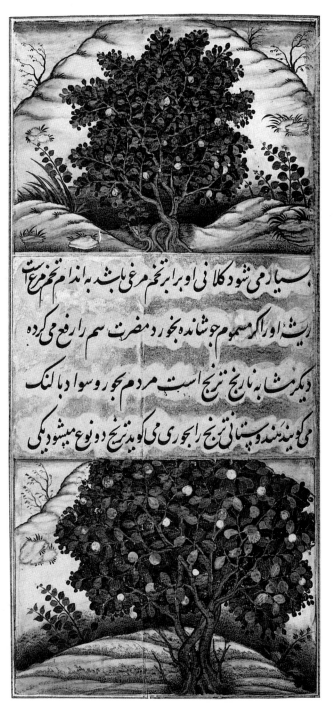

33 *Lime and bitter orange trees, depicted in an Imperial
Mughal manuscript, c.1590. [Or. 3714, f. 404a]*

34 *A lively garden scene from an Imperial Mughal manuscript (1595), with characteristic water channels and pools and a range of garden activities and entertainments.* [Or. 12208, f. 65a]

35 *The Emperor Babur celebrates the birth of his first son, Humayun, in his garden, illustrated in the memoirs of Babur produced under the patronage of the Emperor Akbar, c.1590. As in Iran, Imperial Mughal gardens were often used for public celebrations and receptions.* [Or. 3714, f. 295a]

protection from the sun by an awning. Similar raised platforms situated so that the emperor could overlook the garden, are still in place in the Rambagh at Agra. Babur is being entertained by musicians and dancers while servants bearing gifts are approaching the garden gate in the foreground. Water channels flow into the square tank with its central fountain. As in Iran, gardens were used for celebrations, such as this, and for the reception of diplomats and deputations, for discussions and for entertainment, as well as for rest, coolness and tranquillity. On this occasion Babur wrote of the gifts brought to him, noting also 'it was a first-rate feast'.

Babur died at the end of 1530 and was buried in his garden tomb at Kabul. He was succeeded by Humayun who did not inherit his love of gardens. Humayun died in 1556 as the result of an accident before he had designed his own tomb or chosen a site for it. It was a tradition that the choice of a site, the tomb itself and the design of the gardens surrounding it, were usually begun by the future occupant in his own lifetime. Humayun's widow built the complex at Delhi and it was completed in 1573. The gardens surrounding it are one of the very few Mughal gardens to survive in the original Persian-inspired *chahar bagh* form and they are laid out in a series of *chahar bagh* plans. The parterres are divided by wide paths which have narrow water channels running down the centre. They are arranged on low terraces to provide gravity for a steady flow of water. Later Mughal garden landscape designers developed the water channels on a far larger scale until they resembled canals. They were also constructed on different levels but with deeper terracing, the water flowing from level to level down chutes, cascades and waterfalls.

Akbar, the greatest of the Mughal emperors, succeeded Humayun in 1556 when he was only 13, and reigned until his death in 1605. He was a man of wide interests, although garden landscaping was not such an outstanding passion as it had been for Babur. However, he appreciated Babur's skill and paid tribute to him, noting that he had enhanced India by landscape gardening, wide avenues and falling water. It is due to Akbar's patronage of the arts and of book production that manuscripts copied from the late 16th century at his atélier included the memoirs of Babur which were illustrated with miniatures of superb quality by the imperial artists. Miniatures that include Mughal gardens as subjects or as backgrounds provide invaluable insights, for, besides the layout, they also include details such as plants and trees, oxen working the water wheels to draw water from wells, gardeners' tools and the clay containers for keeping tree roots watered [36].

Chronicles[2] kept by Akbar's officials of the events of his daily life and of state affairs included numerous inventories as well as lists of indigenous trees, plants and flowers with descriptions of their characteristics.

2 Francis Gladwin (translator),
*Ayeen Akbery; or the Institutes of the
Emperor Akbar*, vol. 1 (London,
1800).

36 *A magnificent tree in a clay irrigation container used to keep its roots watered, from the poems of Nizami.*
[Or. 12208, f. 52a]

37 A photograph of Akbar's tomb at Sikandra
(c.1870) showing the central approach and
trees in adjoining courtyards. [IOL 169B (3)]

38 This huge early 19th-century drawing of
Akbar's tomb (left) gives some indication of the
enormous scale of the building and its gardens,
with their courtyards, channels, pools,
fountains and trees. Gardeners at work are
depicted in detail (right), here sweeping up
fallen leaves. [IOL Or. 4202]

Akbar had gardens laid out around the buildings of his new city, Fatehpur Sikri, and at Agra. He conquered Kashmir in 1586 and was entranced by the setting of Lake Dal, with its backdrop of mountains, and by the wild flowers which carpeted the meadows in spring. He built a palace in Kashmir, Nasim Bagh, which was surrounded by gardens. Akbar's tomb at Sikandra, on the plains near Agra, was begun in his own lifetime and completed by his son, Jahangir. It was surrounded by gardens laid out in the *chahar bagh* style, each section divided into four parts divided by raised paths, every one with a central water channel. Fountains, tanks and waterfalls were supplied by wells and water flowed into pools which were used for irrigating the fruit trees, flower beds and avenues. As at the Taj Mahal, fountains were supplied by underground pipes fed from the wells by means of overhead tanks which provided the enormous amount of water required for irrigation and for supplying the channels. The size of this tomb and garden is shown in a huge 19th century drawing which indicates the extent of the gardens, and their courtyards, channels, pools, fountains and trees [37, 38].

Jahangir himself inherited his great-grandfather Babur's interest in the landscaping of gardens and his love of flowers. Kashmir was to remain the area he loved most from the time he accompanied Akbar there. In his memoirs,[3] Jahangir writes about 'mead after mead of flowers. Sweet-smelling plants of narcissus, violet & strange flowers'. Included among the latter was the crown imperial lily which was unfamiliar to Jahangir and which, subsequently, was often included amongst the flower paintings decorating the borders of album and manuscript pages [39]. 'The flowers of Kashmir are beyond counting and calculation,' he wrote, and he commissioned his artist, Mansur, to paint over a hundred of them. Mansur, who specialized in painting flora and fauna, used to accompany Jahangir to Kashmir and was given the title of 'Wonder of the Age' by him. In his memoirs Jahangir describes the beauty of the setting and lists some of the flowers and fruit: 'In the spring the hills and plains are filled with blossoms. Tulips everywhere, almond and peach, *chambili* (white jasmine) and blue jasmine, apricots, lilies, pears, apples, guavas, grapes, pomegranates, water melons, mulberry, cherries.'

3 A. Rogers (translator), *Tuzuk-i Jahangiri; or Memoirs of Jahangir*, ed. H. Beveridge, vols. 1 and 2 (London, 1909, 1914).

39 Crown Imperial lilies and other flowers decorating a manuscript dated 1663. [RAS Persian MS 310, f. 35b]

Jahangir visited Babur's gardens at Kabul, 'seven in one day', and he was supported in his interest by his wife, Nur Jahan, and his brother-in-law, Asaf Khan, who both designed beautiful gardens. During the long periods they spent in Kashmir, the magnificent gardens Vernag [*see* 40, 41], Nishat [*see* 42, 43] and Shalimar were created. In addition, a series of palaces and buildings with gardens were built at the various stopping places, including Sialkot and Rajaur, on the road from Agra to Kashmir, as the emperors would be accompanied by a large entourage of courtiers, soldiers and servants, as well as members of their own families.

Jahangir's ideal garden, described by himself in his memoirs, was one laid out according to his directions in Sihrind which he visited on his way to Kashmir. He wrote that it afforded him the utmost delight: '... on entering the garden, I found myself immediately in a covered avenue, planted on each side with scarlet roses and, beyond them, arose groves of cypress, fir, plane and evergreens ... Passing through these, we entered what was in reality the garden, which now exhibited a variegated parterre ornamented with flowers of the utmost brilliancy of colours and of the choicest kind'. He goes on to describe the reservoir of water in the centre of the green parterre, and the octagonal pavilion which was 'capable of accommodating two hundred persons with convenient room to sit and surrounded by a beautiful colonnade'. Similar to a Persian pavilion, it was two storeys high and decorated with murals.

The garden at Vernag, about 40 miles south of Kashmir, is notable for the large pool fed by springs of the purest water. It was full of fish when Jahangir saw it in the 17th century, as indeed it still is today. Water flows under the arches of the surrounding arcade and eventually into the river Jhelum by way of a 12-foot-wide canal. In Ottoman Turkey lamps and candles were used in gardens to enhance the beauty of the flowers, but in Mughal gardens in India they were placed behind water to create a sparkling effect as waterfalls flowed over them. Holders for lamps and candles were built into niches in the brickwork and can still be seen in the 16th-century Rambagh gardens at Agra. Succeeding Mughal emperors employed them in niches of cascades, waterfalls and pavilions. Buildings round the pool at Vernag were introduced by Jahangir in 1609. It was at Vernag that Jahangir and Nur Jahan spent much of their time and it was his unfulfilled wish to be buried there.

Nishat Bagh, situated on Lake Dal, was a far more ambitious scheme than Vernag. Entered from below, it provides a superb vista, its outstanding feature being a central canal constructed on a series of terraces down which water flows from one level to the next by means of cascades and waterfalls into the lake below. Rows of fountains are placed down the centre of each pool on every level. The central terraced pools are flanked by flower beds and the whole garden surrounded by shady plane trees. On some levels a dais or seat was constructed over the water just above the chute. An illustrated manuscript, produced in Lahore in 1663, of the poems of Zafar Khan, governor of Kashmir, includes miniatures of events taking place in Kashmir gardens. One is of Vernag with its fish pool and arcading [41] and another, with its pavilion, cascade and dais, is almost certainly Nishat Bagh [43]. Of the Shalimar gardens Jahangir wrote: 'Shalimar is near the lake. It has a pleasant stream which comes down from the hills and flows into the Dal Lake. I bade my son [*i.e.* Shahjahan] dam it up and make a waterfall . . . This place is one of the sights of Kashmir.'

Shahjahan, who succeeded his father in 1627, was more interested in architecture than horticulture, and added buildings to existing gardens including a black marble pavilion in the Shalimar. Magnificent buildings dating from his reign included palaces with extensive gardens at Delhi, Lahore and Agra as well as the most famous of all, the Taj Mahal. This tomb was built for his wife Mumtaz Mahal who died in 1631. Following the Mughal tradition it stands in extensive grounds, although these gardens have been altered considerably over the years. The original plan of the garden was conventional, with fountains placed at intervals down the central channel and a large raised pool with a cusped and trefoiled

40 A 19th-century photograph of the sacred pool in the magnificent gardens at Vernag, created during Jahangir's time in Kashmir [see also 41]. [IOL 94/1]

41 *A manuscript painting of the Vernag gardens dated 1663. [RAS Persian MS 310, ff. 31b–32]*

42 *A 19th-century photograph of the site of the cascade at Nishat Bagh. [IOL 556/1 (19)]*

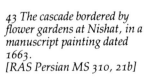

43 The cascade bordered by flower gardens at Nishat, in a manuscript painting dated 1663.
[RAS Persian MS 310, 21b]

border providing wonderful reflections of the building. Water channels at right angles to the main canal divide the garden into the traditional *chahar bagh* scheme. Begun in 1632, it was completed in 1648 and an unusual feature is the positioning of the tomb building at the end of the garden, thus providing an exquisite vista of channels, fountains and reflections. Unlike the long terraced central channel of the Nishat Bagh in Kashmir, which is made spectacular by its series of waterfalls and cascades, the Taj Mahal channel relies on fountains supplied by a sophisticated system of water pipes. The flower beds were planted with roses, tulips, crown imperials, lilies and irises with orchards of mangos, oranges, lemons, pomegranates, apples and guavas. Shady trees such as banyan, plane, cypress, jackfruit and pipal and sweet-scented shrubs including jasmine, champa, oleander and screwpine were widely grown. The flower theme continues in the decorations of semi-precious stones inlaid in the marble of the tomb in the form of sprays, flowers and trees while the outer walls are decorated with flowers in bas-relief.

The Taj Mahal and its garden has been a subject of paintings by Indian and European artists for years. William Daniell painted a version in 1789 of which an aquatint was published in 1801 [*see* 29], whilst an exquisite painting by an Indian artist, dated *c*.1830, appears in a history of Shahjahan [44]. Although it includes somewhat unflattering representations of British officers on the terrace, the painting of the building shows strong European influence.

The concept introduced in the Nishat Bagh, of a pavilion at the far end of a long vista, viewed from below and dominated by a main water channel with waterfalls, chutes and cascades, was reversed during Aurangzib's reign. He succeeded in 1658 and, like Shahjahan, was mainly interested in architecture but, unlike his predecessor, did not create large gardens to accompany his buildings. One who did, however, was his chief architect, Faday Khan, who designed a superb garden at Pinjaur where he was governor. In contrast to the Nishat Bagh, the entrance was positioned above the highest terrace and although planned in the usual way, with a central terraced canal, when it was viewed from above it made nothing like the impact of the Nishat Bagh vista seen from below.

Although gardens were no longer laid out on such a magnificent scale after the decline of the Mughal empire in the 18th century, the tradition was maintained, albeit less ambitiously, by princes and nobles in Central India. They, as well as Mughal governors and high officials, had always taken pleasure in creating gardens for themselves, usually in the *chahar bagh* format, from the late 16th century onwards. They were also patrons of book production and an illustration in a simpler Mughal style, dated 1598, includes a charming and uncomplicated *chahar bagh* [45]. A late

44 *The Taj Mahal at Agra painted by an Indian artist, c.1830.*
[Or. 2157, f. 612a]

45 *An Imperial Mughal miniature, c.1598,*
showing a simple chahar bagh. *[Or. 12076, f. 95a]*

47 A simple chahar bagh *illustrated in a miniature painted in
Hyderabad in 1760. [IOL Johnson 37–2]*

*46 A prince in his garden. This later Mughal miniature (1700)
shows the development of the* chahar bagh *system into a more
complicated scheme of flowerbeds and paths.*
[IOL Johnson 1–29]

48 A delicate Deccani plan of an orchard, c.1685. [Or. 338, f. 110a]

Mughal miniature (dated AD 1700) of a prince being entertained illustrates the development of the garden, over the course of a century, into a more fussy plan with innumerable small flowerbeds surrounded by paths [46]. A garden in a Hyderabad painting of c.1760 is of an altogether simpler design, with its pool, fountain and flanking flower beds [47].

An unusual plan of an orchard included in a British Library manuscript of a poem copied in 1685 in the Deccan, probably at Bijapur, is typical of delicate Deccani paintings. The plan is interesting because the central canal, with its two reservoirs, has no side channels to provide irrigation to the fruit trees. These include fig, mango, pomegranate and citrus, underplanted with poppies, daylilies and narcissus. The channel flows through the gap in the wall and into, or underneath, the end pavilion which has cypresses and willows on either side of it [48].

In the 17th and 18th centuries some of the princely states remained relatively independent of Mughal rule. This is reflected in their art, particularly in illustrated copies of the Hindu epics, including the *Ramayana* and works that relate episodes in the life of Krishna. Some manuscripts were written on palm leaves or aloe bark.[4] Gardens, trees, flowers and the fauna of the forests are interwoven in the stories and, in turn, serve as backgrounds to the illustrations by Hindu artists. Some paintings include Mughal features against a Hindu background as, for example, an illustration in a copy of the Last Book of the *Ramayana* produced for a Hindu patron at Udaipur. Dated 1653, it includes the Mughal garden plan of pool, fountain and channels in simplified form in an otherwise Indian setting [49].

4 J. P. Losty, *The Art of the Book in India* (London, 1982).

49 *The Mughal* chahar bagh *incorporated in an Indian setting, 1653.*
[*Add. 15297 (2), f. 70*]

50 Gopis searching for Krishna in the forest, in a palm leaf manuscript produced in the early 18th century in Orissa. [Or. 11689 (13a)]

51 A natural garden setting full of stylised plants and flowers, illustrating Krishna with the gopas in the forest. An Assamese painting on aloe bark, 1836. [Or. 11387, f. 3a]

The *Bhagavata Purana*, a collection of stories about the incarnation of Vishnu, contains an account of the early life of the god Krishna and the infatuation of the *gopis*, the wives and daughters of the cowherds. During one episode they think Krishna has deserted them and frantically search the forest, calling on the trees and plants by name for help in finding him.[5] In illustrations to this story, on palm-leaves, each of the trees is named and drawn, in a manuscript produced in the early 18th century at Orissa, on the Bay of Bengal [50]. These delicate drawings which were incised on the leaves with a stylus and then coloured, include fig trees (pipal and banyan), sacred basil, sweet-smelling champa, four jasmines, mango, breadfruit, rose apple and other sacred trees, each one named.

An Assamese manuscript dated 1836 is a copy of the *Brahmakanda* written and illustrated on sheets of aloe bark. It includes a painting of a scene in a forest where Krishna is disporting himself with the *gopas* (cow-herds). Crammed with stylised plants and flowers, animals, birds and insects, set amongst rounded rocks, it provides a joyous natural garden setting for the dancers.

5 J. P. Losty, *Krishna: A Hindu Vision of God* (London, 1980).

52 *Kashmiri vegetable growers at work, illustrated with a selection of their tools in a mid-19th century volume.* [IOL Add. Or. 1708]

53 *A gardener making garlands in an early 19th-century painting showing strong European influence.* [Add. 27255, f. 231b]

The crumbling of the Mughal empire and the increasing influence of the British in India in the late 18th and 19th centuries led to gardens being landscaped in a far more English style. Army officers and officials of the East India Company became the patrons of local artists and painting styles became more and more European. One example is a study of a gardener making garlands, one of a series of paintings of castes and occupations commissioned by Colonel James Skinner [53]. The gardener is working in a garden in which a lawn has taken the place of the usual channel. The painting was produced for Skinner in 1825 on his estate at Hansi, 85 miles north-west of Delhi. Another illustration, included in a mid-19th century volume of drawings of trades and occupations in Kashmir, shows a vegetable grower with his implements and examples of vegetables and fruit grown by him; these include rice, radishes, cucumbers, melons, pumpkins, pot-herbs, apples, lotus leaves and flowers and a sheaf of reeds.

Watercolour studies of specimens of Indian flowers and plants by Indian artists were commissioned by Europeans, one of the most notable being the collection formed by William Roxborough, the first official superintendent of the Calcutta Botanic Gardens. European artists, in turn, were commissioned to paint scenes and buildings in India and such artists as Thomas and William Daniell have left valuable records of Indian gardens as they were in the late-18th and 19th centuries.

China

The earliest recorded Chinese gardens were the vast hunting parks of semi-mythical emperors. The wickedness of Jie Gui, last ruler of the Xia dynasty (said to have fallen in c.1763 BC) was expressed in the excesses of his park, where ponds were filled with wine and hunks of meat hung in trees, and the tyrant Zhou, last ruler of the Shang dynasty (which fell in c.1122 BC) was said to have squandered the imperial treasury on parks and gardens where orgies of all sorts took place. The philosopher

54

55 *A lakeside pavilion in the Imperial resort at Chengde, from the Kang xi emperor's poems describing the summer resort, an illustrated copper engraved edition by Matteo Ripa, postface dated 1712. [19957 c.4]*

Mencius (fourth century BC), inheritor of the mantle of Confucius, deplored the excesses of Jie and Zhou and frequently pointed to the lavish construction of gardens as an indicator of the barbarity of a ruler. Pulling down houses to make ponds, seizing fields for parks and depriving peasants of their livelihood were aspects of careless rule.

Later emperors continued the tradition. The great summer palaces of the Qing rulers (1644–1911) are the only survivors of these huge imperial enclosures [55] and their vast area contrasts with the better known aspect of the Chinese garden tradition – the tiny gardens crammed with pools, rocks and pavilions that were constructed by the educated class and those who aspired to elegance [54, 56]. Both of these traditions, together with the gardens that were often constructed in Buddhist temple enclosures [*see* 58], had an overwhelming influence on the development of the Japanese garden.

54 Some typical elements of Chinese small-garden design: a pavilion with piled rocks and a tree beside a lotus pool. A scene from the life of Meng jiang nu, the woman whose tears made the Great Wall crumble. Chinese coloured woodblock 'New Year' print, early 20th century. [Or. 5896] 71

56 'Pan Khaqua's garden', a Cantonese export watercolour showing plants in pots and garden buildings, 19th century. [IOL Add. Or. 2127]

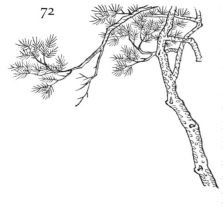

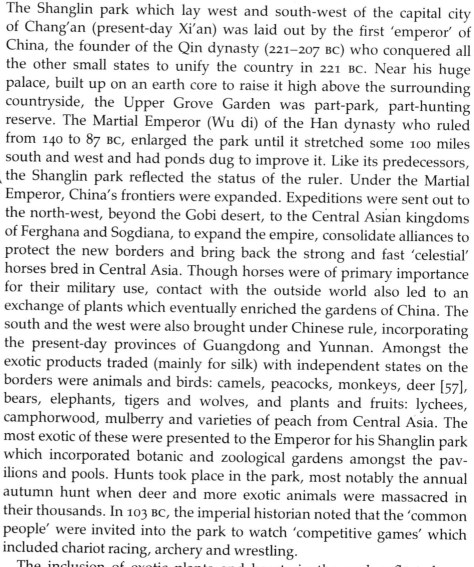

The Shanglin park which lay west and south-west of the capital city of Chang'an (present-day Xi'an) was laid out by the first 'emperor' of China, the founder of the Qin dynasty (221–207 BC) who conquered all the other small states to unify the country in 221 BC. Near his huge palace, built up on an earth core to raise it high above the surrounding countryside, the Upper Grove Garden was part-park, part-hunting reserve. The Martial Emperor (Wu di) of the Han dynasty who ruled from 140 to 87 BC, enlarged the park until it stretched some 100 miles south and west and had ponds dug to improve it. Like its predecessors, the Shanglin park reflected the status of the ruler. Under the Martial Emperor, China's frontiers were expanded. Expeditions were sent out to the north-west, beyond the Gobi desert, to the Central Asian kingdoms of Ferghana and Sogdiana, to expand the empire, consolidate alliances to protect the new borders and bring back the strong and fast 'celestial' horses bred in Central Asia. Though horses were of primary importance for their military use, contact with the outside world also led to an exchange of plants which eventually enriched the gardens of China. The south and the west were also brought under Chinese rule, incorporating the present-day provinces of Guangdong and Yunnan. Amongst the exotic products traded (mainly for silk) with independent states on the borders were animals and birds: camels, peacocks, monkeys, deer [57], bears, elephants, tigers and wolves, and plants and fruits: lychees, camphorwood, mulberry and varieties of peach from Central Asia. The most exotic of these were presented to the Emperor for his Shanglin park which incorporated botanic and zoological gardens amongst the pavilions and pools. Hunts took place in the park, most notably the annual autumn hunt when deer and more exotic animals were massacred in their thousands. In 103 BC, the imperial historian noted that the 'common people' were invited into the park to watch 'competitive games' which included chariot racing, archery and wrestling.

The inclusion of exotic plants and beasts in the park reflected one aspect of imperial garden planning which was to impress Japanese visitors some 500 years later. Filled with the produce of the empire, the park served as a miniature version of the empire. Its wooded hills and pools were the mountains and rivers with their natural inhabitants. In another of his gardens surrounding the capital, the Martial Emperor expanded on the same theme in his lake park. Three small islands in the lake were named after the mythical islands of the immortals which were supposed to lie off the coast of Shandong province. Immortals in Chinese belief were people who through various magical practices had managed to avoid death. Though Taoism is commonly regarded as a philosophical system idealising harmony between nature and man, one sect of Taoists in the Han dynasty developed a whole series of practices including

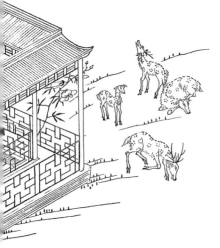

57 Animals were a common feature of Chinese gardens from the days of the earliest imperial parks onwards, and the pool here was especially dug for these deer. From an illustration in Hong xue yin yuan, *the illustrated autobiography of Linqing.* [15292, f. 1/4]

breathing exercises and the ingestion of (dangerous) potions in the search for physical immortality and eternal life on the islands. The Martial Emperor consulted the leading Taoists about his own immortality and the tall pavilions and halls on the rocky, wooded islands which rose from the lake were said to have been constructed in an attempt to lure immortals inland so that he might learn their secrets. It is not surprising that wealthy merchants of the Han copied the imperial parks for themselves. Yuan Guanghan diverted streams, built up islands of sand in the resulting pool, constructed pavilions and covered walks and stocked his park with yaks, white parrots and mandarin ducks. Executed for his presumption, his animals and plants were transferred to the imperial Shanglin park.

The second ruler of the Sui dynasty (AD 589–618) built a great garden outside his capital at Luoyang. Continuing the tradition of creating miniature islands of immortals established by the Martial Emperor, he had three islands built and covered with pavilions in the middle of the vast lake in the centre of his park. The enclosure was 75 miles in circumference and stocked with golden monkeys, deer and fine trees seized from neighbouring estates. 'Water palaces' lined the pools and dragon-headed barges filled with orchestras of concubines drifted on the lakes between the unfading flowers of artificial lotuses. In winter, when the maple leaves had fallen, tiny silk flowers were tied amongst the bare branches, a practice that is continued to this day in Peking parks. This garden came to the attention of Ono no Imoko, Japanese envoy to the Sui court and is thought to have been part of the inspiration behind the first

58 The Long tan *or Dragon pool in one of the major temples outside Peking, famous for its great black carp. The pool is walled and the walls pierced with ornamental openings typical of Chinese garden architecture. From the illustrated autobiography of a Qing official, Linqing,* Hong xue yin yuan tu qi *(Tracks of a wild swan in the snow), 1847–1850. [15292 f. 1/6]*

Japanese imperial parks in the early seventh century. Though the construction of islands in a lake 'sea' continued to play an important part in Japanese garden design, this form of symbolic representation on the grand scale gradually fell out of favour in China and most subsequent imperial parks, whilst still filled with lakes, islands and pavilions, took their inspiration from landscape painting and the small gardens of the south rather than oceans, islands of the blessed and imaginary worlds.

Wall paintings in tombs of the Tang dynasty (AD 618–907) depict gentlemen in black ear-flapped hats and short gowns mounted on fat horses with their tails tied in stumpy plaits, playing polo. Some show ladies in loose gowns seated on rocks beneath leafy trees. Polo was played in the imperial parks of the Tang, whilst more elaborate gardens were constructed for imperial favourites. At the Huaqing springs outside the capital where hot water bubbles endlessly into a series of pools beneath green wooded mountain slopes, the Dark Emperor (Xuan zong) who reigned from 712–756, improved the existing gardens, setting up a miniature island of lapis lazuli in the pool where court ladies floated in lacquered boats, and constructing a marble bath for his famously fat concubine, Yang Guifei. The Huaqing hot springs are still in use and lotuses flower at the corners of the square pool where court ladies boated: 'Amongst the dense lotus flowers, a small boat drifts, Looking for her lover she nods her head and smiles, A green jade hairpin falls into the water'.[1]

Earlier in the Tang, the Empress Wu was the first ruler to establish a 'summer palace' in hills north of the capital where she would decamp

1 Arthur Waley, *The Life and Times of Po Chü-i* (London, Allen and Unwin, 1949).

59 Winter-flowering narcissus, camellia and prunus from Jie zi yuan hua juan (*Colour prints from the Mustard Seed Garden painting manual), Chinese coloured woodblock, c.1679–1791.* [15274 a. 1]

with the entire court to escape the heat of the plains. Such 'summer palaces' were to be built in considerable numbers by the later emperors of the Qing (1644–1911) who also moved the court every summer. The Empress Wu's courtiers complained bitterly about the upheaval, especially as they had to live in straw huts in the rural retreat. The desire for escape from the summer heat was also evident in another of the Dark Emperor's garden buildings, the Cool Hall. Surrounded by fountains forming walls of water, cool air was blown in by fan-wheels operated by the movement of water. The seats were cooled by blocks of ice and iced drinks were served.

Disapproval of lavish imperial spending on gardens continued: the poet Bai Juyi, a garden-lover on a small scale, lamented the fate of the elephants in the imperial menagerie whose poor condition due to neglect he contrasted with the tender care lavished on them during the glorious reign of the founder of the Tang dynasty. Bai Juyi's poems are full of garden-related images: as a government official, kept up all night on duty in the palace, he wrote of the stillness of the pines and bamboos in the palace courtyards and when he was serving as governor of Zhongzhou in Sichuan province, he spent his money on fruit trees for the eastern embankment: 'I simply bought whatever had most blooms, not caring

60 A pine and rock in a typical garden grouping, from Shi zhu zhai shu hua pu (Colour prints from the Ten Bamboo Studio). A Chinese coloured woodblock print, Nanjing, c.1643. [Or. 59 a. 10]

whether peach, apricot or plum ... The red flowers hang like a heavy mist, the white flowers gleam like a fall of snow ... In front there flows an ever-running stream, beneath a little terrace ...'2

His poems contain references to exotic animals like the red cockatoo ('sent as a present from Annam') and those of Du Fu (712–70) describe yet another Tang imperial garden built for the fat concubine, Yang Guifei, where she buried her white cockatoo with coral feet in a burial mound with a proper Buddhist funeral service. Here the customary lake with its three 'islands of the immortals' was overlooked by a terrace planted with peonies, the most fashionable flower of the period.

One of the great imperial garden-builders was the Honorable Emperor (Hui zong) of the Song who reigned from 1101 to 1126 and saw the division of China and the loss of the north to 'barbarian invaders', a disaster which some attributed, as Mencius might have done, to his lavish spending on his garden. Like previous imperial parks, this contained the requisite menagerie with golden pheasants and deer of all

61 The fashion for collecting rocks has been a longstanding feature of Chinese garden design. The varied and ancient rocks in the celebrated Half-Acre Garden taken over by the Qing official, Linqing, were said to have been selected and arranged by Li Yu (1611–1680?), a dramatist and poet, also the designer of the famous Mustard Seed garden in Nanjing [see 59]. From Hong xue yin yuan, the illustrated autobiography of Linqing. [15292, f. 1/5]

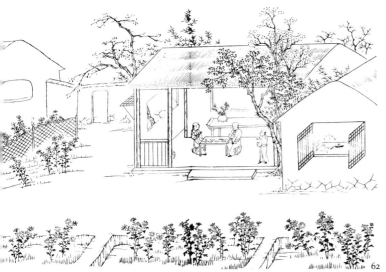

sorts and exotic plants like the southern lychee. The park was dominated by the Gen yue or Eastern Peak on whose summit stood a terrace where the emperor could view his capital. The massed rocks forming the Eastern Peak were dotted with curiously shaped stones and lake rocks, 'in various strange shapes, like tusks, horns, mouths, noses, heads, tails and claws', and amongst them were equally contorted pines, their trunks and branches twisted into the form of dragons, cranes and auspicious characters. In his passion for collecting strangely shaped rocks, the 'petromaniac' emperor was reflecting a contemporary craze, which had begun in the ninth century. Travellers, particularly those who ventured to the frontiers of the far south where strange 'forests' of worn limestone peaks dominated the landscape, helped to create the fashion. Vast sums were spent on transporting bizarre rocks ('the best of these were eroded limestone crags')[2] to the gardens of aristocrats and emperors. Li Deyu, a magistrate resident in Luoyang, wrote that he had no need to visit famous mountains for he had his own 'cluster of peaks' in his garden at home [61]. The Honourable Emperor of the Song despatched 'rock convoys' all over China, blocking the Grand Canal and disrupting the movement of the essential grain barges; one of the stones destined for his Eastern Peak, was the Exquisite Jade Rock, now in the Yu yuan (Mandarin Garden) in Shanghai. On its way to the capital, the boat in which it was being transported sank in a storm on the Huangpu river near the small county town which later grew into the city of Shanghai. In the 16th century, when an official called Pan Yunduan was designing a garden for his father, he had the river dredged to recover the Exquisite Jade Rock. Its pitted surface, described as 'crapy, scraggy and holey'[3] is characteristic of the desired type, as is its form. Swelling from a very narrow base, it appears to defy gravity.

Beneath the Eastern Peak, plum and apricot trees were planted in great numbers so that, in spring, the mountain seemed to rise out of a cloud of

62 Discussing philosophy in the rustic hut of a chrysanthemum expert, surrounded by flowers grown in sunken beds. From Hong xue yin yuan, the illustrated autobiography of Linqing. [15292, f. 1/2]

63 Writing poems in praise of flowers in the Phoenix tower, with a gnarled tree, a willow and a raised bed for inspiration. From Hong xue yin yuan, the illustrated autobiography of Linqing. [152292, f. 1/1]

2 Edward Schaeffer, *The Vermilion Bird* (Berkeley, University of California Press, 1967).

3 Pan Ling, *In Search of Old Shanghai* (Hong Kong, Joint Publishing Company, 1982).

blossom. Pools and buildings clustered at the foot of the mountain which was approached by a road lined with further prizes of the 'rock convoys'. Many of these were personally named by the Emperor, their titles carved in gold letters. The same fondness for naming stones, for seeing elephants, water buffalo, paired swans and human figures in their gnarled forms, continues today. Inscriptions cover the rocks in the gardens on Tiger Hill outside Suzhou and the strange peaks of the limestone 'Stone Forest' near Kunming. Visitors will strain to identify the characteristics of the rocks that have inspired their names and, at the same time, admire the varied calligraphy (one of the most highly regarded art forms in China) that contributes to the interest of the scene.

After the 12th-century invasion of Kaifeng, the Eastern Peak, symbol of imperial unconcern, was destroyed by local inhabitants. The capital of the Song was moved south to the city of Hangzhou, long famous for its beautiful natural scenery. The city lies beside the West Lake (Xi hu) which is surrounded by low wooded hills and is perhaps the best example of a natural landscape that has been constantly embellished by

64 A garden in spring illustrating all the major features of a southern garden; also famous as a site commemorated in a poem by Su Dongpo (1036–1101). From an album of paintings illustrating the stations of the Qian long emperor's fifth tour of inspection in South China; the last painting is signed by Qian Weicheng (1720–72). [Or. 12895]

man. Man's position in nature and his hand in it is not an explicit theory but it lies behind many aspects of Chinese culture. The holy mountains of the Chinese Buddhists are dotted with temples and pretty pavilions where pilgrims can rest and admire a spectacular waterfall or a twisted pine beside a pointed peak; Chinese landscape paintings very frequently include a rustic hut from where the painter views towering mountains and most Chinese nature poetry includes the poet in the landscape, firmly shutting his wicket gate against unwanted guests so that he can play his zither, drink wine and converse with the moon [62, 63]. Though the Taoists held that nature had its own pattern, to which man should conform and not attempt to alter the inherent balance, the scenery of Hangzhou offers a long history of improvements. To the north and east, long dykes run across the edges of the West Lake: the Bai causeway with a humped stone bridge (Jade Belt Bridge) links the largest of the four islands in the lake to the shore and it is named after the poet Bai Juyi, governor of Hangzhou in 822–25. Bai Juyi did carry out improvements to the lake although he did not, in fact, construct this causeway.

65 'The Ambassador's residence at Canton', showing the garden with rocks, pavilion and pool. Watercolour by William Alexander, 1794. [IOL 959, f. 36/17]

The longer Su causeway with its six small bridges was built by another great poet, Su Dongpo, who also served as governor of Hangzhou in the 11th century. It was built out of silt dredged up from the lake and another of his innovations was the erection of stone lanterns in the lake, set in the deepest part marking the area where it was forbidden to grow any water plants (in an attempt to reduce silting). Lit up at night with candles, together with the moon, they create the illusion of four moons reflected in the water. Such stone lanterns are still an important part of Japanese garden planning; here they survive as an isolated example of what must once have been a fashionable garden feature in China.

The wooded hills surrounding the lake conceal a number of fine temples but were also embellished by free-standing pagodas. Pagodas, ostensibly very Chinese buildings, grew from two origins: the brick or stone *stupas* that were an integral part of Indian Buddhist temples, and the free-standing timber towers built for both defensive and decorative purposes during the Han. Though still often associated with Buddhist temples, pagodas were eventually built as solitary monuments, often set up on hills overlooking towns, for it was believed that they could improve the 'wind and water' or geomancy of an area, preventing floods and other disasters. Multi-eaved, often with upturned eaves and wind-chimes, they are extremely decorative and are perhaps the most common elements in the Chinese garden planning technique of 'borrowing a view', whereby a feature outside a small garden is made the focus of a view from within the garden itself [66, 67]. The West Lake used to be embellished by two pagodas, the Thunder Peak pagoda to the south, which was built in 975 but crashed to the ground in 1925, and the Bao shu (Protector of Virtue) pagoda to the north, first built in 986 which still stands. Printed guidebooks of the 17th and 18th centuries with illustrations of the West Lake all depict a mixture of the natural and the man-made: pagodas above slopes planted with flowering trees, small pavilions and halls on the islands amongst clumps of bamboo and pleasure-boats dotting its surface.

The greatest 'garden' in Song Hangzhou was the West Lake which was open to the public, and the remaining Song emperors, who lived in a huge palace on its shore, made use of the same facility. According to an account recorded in Marco Polo's *Travels*, the emperors had a large park on the lake shore filled with fallow deer, roe deer, red deer, hares and rabbits which they and their concubines would chase with dogs. Heated by the chase, the concubines would then cool off by swimming in the lake whilst the emperor watched from a silk-covered barge.

The Mongols, who finally conquered the whole of China in 1279, were not, despite Coleridge's imaginative description in *Khubla Khan*, garden builders. Khubilai Khan (1215–94) built his new capital at Peking on the

Chinese model, retaining his earlier stronghold of Shangdu (the 'upper capital' and Coleridge's Xanadu) as a hunting preserve where he could pursue the deer and exercise his falcons. Adopting Chinese plans, there was a lake park in Peking, to the north and west of the imperial palace, which survives today as the Bei hai or North Sea Park. This was largely remodelled by the Qing emperors, filled with pavilions and a number of Buddhist temples, including the great white Tibetan *stupa* which dominates the lake.

It was natural for the horseman-emperor Khubilai to prefer his hunting parks in the Mongol homeland but more surprising that the succeeding dynasty whose name was Ming ('bright'), which was established by a Chinese in 1368, did not see any grand imperial garden construction. The extraordinary character who became the founder of the Ming, Zhu Yuanzhang, rose from a background of extreme poverty and deprivation; his immediate successors were preoccupied with securing their frontiers, and later Ming emperors seem to have become bogged down in the paperwork of government, none having the time or the inclination for relaxation in a vast hunting park. It was another non-Chinese imperial family, the Manchus, who founded the Qing dynasty in 1644, who revived the early imperial tradition of great hunting parks.

Three 'summer palaces' are associated with the Qing emperors. The earliest was the mountain village 'where you can escape the heat' (Bi shu shan zhuang) at Chengde, in the mountains about 90 miles north-east of Peking. In a vast valley with a large natural lake (swelled by melting

66 Waiting in a tower for the moon: the elegant belvedere rising above the trees was built for moon viewing. From Xia Xianggeng, Shao you yuan er shi si xiao zhao tu (Twenty-four pictures of Wu Xinfu's 'Almost non-existent' garden), 1815. [15323b . 15, ff. 42–43]

67 Watching a fisherman in a straw raincoat: the perfect illustration of a garden with a 'borrowed view'. The lake lies outside the garden but is visible, complete with rustic boat, from the upper storey of the house. From Xia Xianggeng, Shao you yuan er shi si xiao zhao tu (Twenty-four pictures of Wu Xinfu's 'Almost non-existent' garden). [15323. b. 15, ff. 12–13]

68 The imperial library Wen hui ge (Literary assemblage) in Yangzhou. Seven sets of the 36,000 volume imperial manuscript collectanea Si ku quan shu (Complete collection of the four storehouses) were produced in the late 18th century and stored in specially-built libraries based on a private library in Ningbo. The surrounding garden incorporated fire-preventing features: a bare rockery near the building and a surrounding pool. From Hong xue yin yuan, the illustrated autobiography of Linqing. [15292, f. 1/4]

snow), the Kang xi ('Vigorous and splendid') emperor began the construction of his summer retreat in 1703. A wall some 12 miles long surrounded a park filled with wooded hills to the west, a lake to the east and a small area of courtyard living quarters to the south (though these are low and quite simple, they hardly constitute the humble mountain village for which they are named). The lake, filled with lotuses in summer, frozen hard all winter, has a number of small islands in it and is surrounded by Chinese pavilions and halls, one built specially to house one copy of the vast imperial collectanea, *Si ku quan shu* (Complete treasury of the four storehouses), a manuscript which ran to some 36,000 volumes [68].

As befitted an emperor descended from horsemen, the park was kept stocked with animals for the hunt, most notably the strange Père David deer. Named Elaphurus Davidianus after its discoverer, Armand David (1826–1900), a French Lazarist missionary and naturalist, to the Chinese the deer were known as 'four differences' (*si bu xiang*): their horns are like those of a deer yet they are not deer, they have horse heads but are not horses, donkey's bodies but are not donkeys and their hoofs are like those of cattle but they are not cattle. First seen by their discoverer in 1865, the last of the Chinese herd escaped from the deserted summer palace in 1900 whereupon they were eaten by the starving populace.

Cared for and bred in captivity in England by the Dukes of Bedford, a herd was returned to the park in 1987.

It was in the gardens of the Summer Palace at Chengde that Lord Macartney, the first British Ambassador to China, met the Qian long emperor in 1792. Macartney's secretary, John Barrow, described the approach to the park as much resembling the approach to Luton Hoo in Bedfordshire, 'the grounds gently undulated and checkered with various groups of well-contrasted trees' and the lake and its surroundings, viewed from a 'magnificent yacht'.[4] The islands were differentiated, '. . . one marked by a pagoda or other building, one quite destitute of ornament; some smooth and level, some steep and uneven; others frowning with wood, or smiling with culture'. Later, the embassy was taken to the wooded western part of the park: 'It is one of the finest forest scenes in the world; wild, woody, mountainous and rocky, abounding

4 John Barrow, *Travels in China* (London, 1804).

69 A western view of a corner of a Chinese garden, with piled rocks, bamboo and lotus grown in a jar, in a watercolour by William Alexander, 1793–94. [IOL 959, f. 17/87]

with stags and deer of different species and most of the other beasts of
the chase, not dangerous to man'. Barrow was a discriminating observer,
and he noted one of the fundamental principles of later Chinese garden
design, the importance of garden buildings: 'One thing I was particularly
struck with, I mean the happy choice of situation for ornamental
buildings. From attention to this circumstance they have not the air of
being crowded or disproportioned; they never intrude upon the eye; but
wherever they appear they always show themselves to advantage, and
aid, improve, and enliven the prospect.' He was more critical of some
details, confessing that he did 'not much admire' the lotuses that filled
the lake. 'Artificial rocks and ponds with gold and silver fish are perhaps
too often introduced, and the monstrous porcelain figures of lions and
tigers, usually placed before the pavilions, are displeasing to an European eye; but these are trifles of no great moment . . .'

Nearer Peking, two further Summer Palaces were built by the Qing
emperors. The Qian long (Surpassing sovereign) emperor (reigned
1736–96) oversaw the construction of the most extraordinary imperial
garden, the Yuan ming yuan or Garden of Perfect Brightness, in the
mid-18th century. Fundamentally a Chinese garden on the grand scale,
with garden buildings set amongst hills and pools, the garden was
described by the Jesuit Attiret in 1743, 'Hills have been constructed, 50 to
60 feet high, creating an infinity of small valleys between them. Water is
conducted through a number of artificial channels, and collected in many
spots to form pools and lakes. One travels the pools, lakes and canals in
magnificent barges . . . in all the valleys, beside the water are beautifully
grouped assortments of buildings: courtyards, halls, galleries, gardens
and waterfalls . . . You move from one valley to another, not along a
straight path as in Europe but by zig-zags, winding paths, themselves
adorned with little pavilions and grottoes through which you reach
another valley, quite different from the first, distinguished by its con-
tours or the form of its buildings.'[5] He also noted the preference for
flowering trees on the slopes [70] and the cunning design of the canals,
bordered with rough 'natural' stones and winding through rocks and
hills, quite the reverse of the neatly bordered, straight waterways of
French gardens of the period. Amongst this grand Chinese landscape,
were a group of surprising buildings, the 'European palaces' built
between 1740 and 1747 by a group of Jesuit specialists, including the
famous painter Guiseppe Castiglione (1688–1766) who designed the
Italianate buildings and Father Michel Benoist (1715–74) who designed
the fountain which cast its water into a great stone shell (one of the few
surviving pieces).

Castiglione's edifices were in a kind of Chinese baroque; rusticated
walls were adorned with columns whose embellishment did not quite

5 *Lettres edifiantes et curieuses . . .
par des missionaires Jesuites* (Paris,
Garnier-Flammarion, 1979).

accord with the established orders, as they had swags of stone-carved flowers twisted around them. Such European palaces had no place in the Chinese tradition save to emphasize the grandeur and omnipotence of the emperor; where the Martial emperor of the Han had miniature seas and islands of the immortals, the Qing emperors took European styles into a garden, in a reverse of the fashion for 'Chinoiserie' that was sweeping through Europe at the time, with 'Chinese' gardens at Stowe and a pagoda in Kew Gardens.

The summer palace at Chengde survived, though it was largely abandoned by the later Qing emperors, for after the Excellent and Blessed Emperor (Jia qing) was killed by a bolt of lightning there in 1820, it was considered to be ill-omened; the Garden of Perfect Brightness was destroyed by British and French troops in 1860 in a campaign intended as a show of strength over the Taiping rebellion. The neighbouring summer palace now known as the Garden of the Cultivation of Peace (Yi he yuan) was also sacked (and suffered further depredations at the hands of foreign troops in 1900 after the Boxer uprising) but was twice rebuilt by the notorious and probably murderous Dowager Empress Ci Xi (whose name means 'motherly and auspicious').

There had been imperial parks on this site, in the northwestern suburbs of Peking, since the 12th century but it was the Qian long

70 Flowering trees on the slopes: prunus with characteristic spring flowers, magnolia and peony, grouped beside a house. From Hong xue yin yuan, *the illustrated autobiography of Linqing.* [15292, f. 1/2]

emperor who relaid the park and extended the lake in honour of his mother's sixtieth birthday in 1750. He had previously used the lake for overseeing naval manoeuvres but decided later to improve it, by adding a 17-arched stone bridge in imitation of the dykes on the West Lake at Hangzhou. Almost all the palaces, pavilions and temples he constructed on the great hill that overlooks the lake were given poetic names associated with his veneration of his mother's great age: the Hall of Goodwill and Longevity, Palace of Joy in Longevity and the Palace of Virtue and Harmony. Behind the hill, he had a mock 'town' created with stone-lined canals imitating the 'Venice of the East', the southern town of Suzhou, which his mother loved. To the east of the hill was a small enclosed garden with a lotus pool at its centre and covered walks and verandahed buildings all round. The Garden of Harmonious Interest (Xie qu yuan) was a reasonably accurate copy of the Garden of Ease (Ji chang yuan) in another southern city, Wuxi, which the emperor had been much impressed by on one of his tours of inspection of South China. All these imitations of southern gardens and scenes mark a distinct departure from the mythical landscapes of the early imperial parks. The growth of importance of the Yangtse Delta in the Ming and Qing in particular had also seen the widespread creation of smaller private gardens [71]. Far from the grand hunting parks of the earlier emperors with their oceans and islands, these were tranquil miniatures, tiny landscapes (sometimes actually designed by painters). The Qing emperors had access to these gardens through their great trips south; whilst inspecting economic progress, they were lodged with their entourage in 'travelling palaces' constructed around the lake at Hangzhou or in specially constructed house-garden complexes characteristic of the Yangtse Delta. On return to the northern capital of Peking, they copied these small, jewel-like enclosures, setting them up amongst the temples and theatres of their grand parks.

The imperial interest in the small gardens of the Yangtse Delta was assisted by the eagerness of the local inhabitants to show off the best of the local style when providing lodgings for the imperial court. One of China's greatest novelists, Cao Xueqin (c.1715–63) was the grandson of Cao Yin (1618–1712), Superintendent of the Imperial Silk Factory in Suzhou, who was responsible for lodging the Kang xi emperor on his tours of inspection of the south in 1699, 1703, 1705 and 1707. To do so, he had a garden palace constructed next door to the factory. Though the construction took place before Cao Xueqin's birth, its scale and magnificence must have entered family folklore for it forms the basis of one of the chapters in Cao Xueqin's great novel *Hong Lou Meng* (usually translated as the Dream of the Red Chamber).[6]

In the novel, when an imperial consort was due to visit Nanjing, the

6 Cao Xueqin, *The Story of the Stone*, translated by David Hawkes (Harmondsworth, Penguin, 1973).

head of the Jia family constructed apartments for her and a lavish garden. Entered through a five-bay gatehouse of plain polished timbers with finely carved lattice windows which stood on a marble platform carved with passion flowers, the garden proper was screened from view by a 'miniature mountain' dotted with 'rugged white rocks resembling monsters and beasts, some recumbent, some rampant, dappled with moss or hung about with creepers, a narrow zig-zag path just discernible between them'. The path led to a 'ravine, green with magnificent trees and ablaze with rare flowers. A clear stream welling up where the trees were thickest wound its way through clefts in the rocks. Some paces further north, on both sides of a level clearing, rose towering pavilions, whose carved rafters and splendid balustrades were half-hidden by the trees' and which overlooked a pool. 'This was enclosed by marble balustrades and spanned by a stone bridge ornamented with the heads of beasts with gaping jaws. On the bridge was a little pavilion.' Further on, 'a cobbled

71 The famous 'Half Acre' garden, laid out in the early 17th century and later inhabited by the Qing official, Linqing, illustrating many traditional features of the Chinese garden: ornamental openings in walls, trees, mock mountain rockery, a pool, potted plants and a garden pavilion. From Hong xue yin yuan, the illustrated autobiography of Linqing. [15292, f. 1/5]

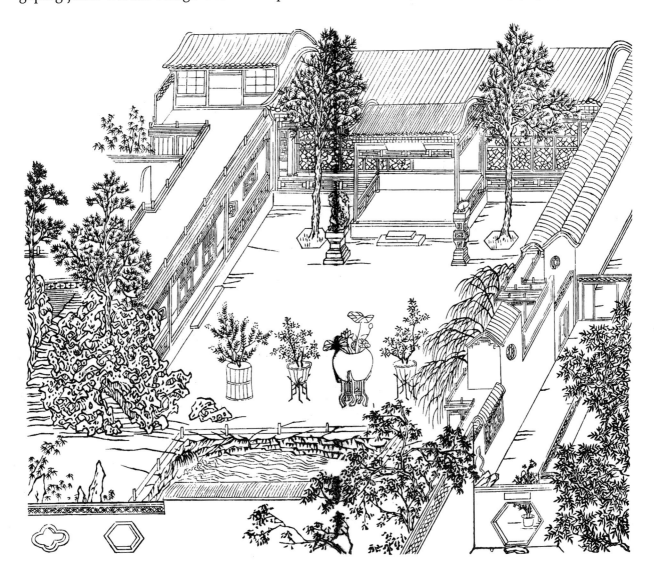

path wound up to a little cottage of three rooms ... a small door ... opened on to the back garden with its large pear-tree, broad-leafed plantain and two tiny side courts ... a brook meandered out through the bamboos.' Other scenes in the garden, revealed as paths turned around rocks and pavilions, included 'double-flowering peach in blossom' and 'a moon gate made of bamboo over which climbed flowering plants'. The balance of plants, water in various forms, buildings and rocks, arranged in a series of concealed views, is characteristic of the private gardens of the south. As one character remarks on leaving the gate-house, 'If not for this hill, one would see the whole garden as soon as one entered and how tame that would be.'

The point of the chapter in which this description occurs is not to describe the garden in prose but to watch the hero of the novel, Baoyu, putting the finishing touch to the whole by finding poetic names and quotations to be inscribed on rocks and lintels [72]. As her host remarked, 'By rights, we should ask the Imperial Consort to do us the honour of composing the inscriptions but she can hardly do this without having seen the place. On the other hand, if we leave the chief sights and pavilions without a single name or couplet until her visit, the garden, however lovely with its flowers and willows, rocks and streams, cannot fully reveal its charm.' The names were not directly descriptive but allusive, making a trip through the garden something of a crossword puzzle as visitors tried to fathom the references. In the largest surviving garden in Suzhou, the Zhuo zheng yuan or 'Garden of the Humble Administrator', a name which, like the imperial 'mountain village' hardly hints at its extravagant extent, the Hall of Distant Fragrance takes its name from the line, 'a distant fragrance is all the more pure' in a Song poem by Zhou Dunyi, 'In praise of the lotus', for the hall stands in front of a lotus-filled pool. Nearby is the Leaning Jade Verandah, beside which bamboos were clumped and described by the painter and poet Wen Zhengming (1470–1559), 'Leaning against the columns, a thousand jade green bamboo stems'. In the same garden, an inscription in the Fan pavilion reads 'With whom shall I sit in the verandah', taken from a poem by Su Dongpo, where the refrain continues 'with the bright moon and a light breeze'. In the Liu Yuan, Garden to Linger In, above a stone doorway is carved an inscription which reads 'Green bamboo by the eastern mountains' and through the doorway a single white lake rock stands in a courtyard planted with bamboo, announced by the inscription.

The importance of literary texts did not only lie in their significance as the finishing touch: literary accounts of great private gardens of the past and the poetic ideal of retreat were also significant. The great growth of private gardens seems to date from the period of disunion after the fall

72 Choosing poetic names and quotations to be inscribed on rocks and lintels. From Cao Xueqin's novel Hong lou meng (Dream of the red chamber), c.1880. [15326 d. 5]

of the Han in 220 BC. Until the empire was reunited in 580, China was divided amongst frequently warring kingdoms. After the certainty of the Han when the centralized bureaucracy, taking its moral justification and guidelines from Confucian texts, the period of disunion was one of introspection and retreat from the unpleasant realities. Buddhism, a religion of rejection of worldly values, made great strides and cultured gentlemen eschewed the civil service, preferring to gather together in rural retreats, drinking and writing poetry. The 'Seven sages of the bamboo grove' of the third century developed the Taoist ideas of the supremacy of nature and man's small part in the great scheme: the Ruan family of poets accepted their pigs as convivial drinking companions and another member of the group was always accompanied by his servant carrying a spade so that he could be buried should he happen to die in the Bamboo Grove; in south China, the great calligrapher and poet Wang Xizhi (321–79) gathered friends outside Shaoxing to drink and write poetry in a garden setting. One of China's greatest poets, Tao Qian (365–427) who abandoned an official career to take up farming, wrote of his retreat from city life: 'A caged bird longs for its native forests . . . Now

73 A rustic retreat: a 'crazy' pool in the Tanzhe temple outside Peking. Built to imperial order the temple includes a replica of a pool designed for a garden game where guests float wine cups on the water and are compelled to compose a line of poetry as a cup floats by them (or pay the forfeit of drinking it). The game was 'invented' by the calligrapher Wang Xizhi (321–379) at the Orchid Pavilion outside Shaoxing. From Hong xue yin yuan, *the illustrated autobiography of Linqing. [152992, f. 1/5]*

74 *Appreciating snow in the garden. Fur coats, charcoal braziers and hot wine around the frozen pool. From* Hong xue yin yuan, *the illustrated autobiography of Linqing.* [15292, f. 1/4]

I shall clear the land at the edge of the southern wilderness, Embracing simplicity, return to garden and field . . . My thatched hut of eight or nine bays, Elms and willows shade the eaves at the rear, Peach and plum trees planted before the hall . . . I return to nature.'⁷

A later character who took the same attitude was Sima Guang (1020–86). Dismissed from office, he retired to write the major historical work *Zi zhi tong jian* (Comprehensive mirror of the art of government) and construct his Garden of Solitary Enjoyment. The garden was near Luoyang which is still famous for its peonies and these were included in the garden although the squared herb plots (rather like Elizabethan box planting) and the 'tents' and 'houses' he constructed by planting bamboo in circles and squares and tying the tops together, excited more interest. They are clearly depicted in a painting, The Garden of Solitary Delight by Qiu Ying (*c.*1494–1552) which was based on Sima Guang's clear account of his work.

The great private gardens of the Ming and Qing, constructed in the pretty towns of the Yangtse Delta, were made for officials and rich

7 My translation but *see* Arthur Waley, *170 Chinese poems* (London, Constable, 1918).

merchants who sought 'the joy of mountain and stream, forest and spring' whilst retaining the material pleasures and resources of the city. Unlike the great imperial parks which were generally constructed outside the city walls, these private gardens were built as functional extensions of town houses [74, 75, 76]. Halls to hold banquets for friends in the garden, extra courtyards, stages for theatrical performances, studios to read or paint in, tall pavilions to admire a distant view, all these were constructed in a garden adjacent to the family house which usually occupied about half the available space. Though retired officials and painters must have taken a personal interest in the construction of their gardens, upwardly mobile merchants, keen to acquire all the trappings of

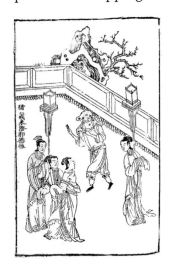

75

76

scholarly elegance, employed garden designers and resorted to a manual of elegant garden design such as the 17th century *Yuan ye* (Craft of Gardens) by Ji Cheng, which, like other 'style manuals' of the period, tended to didactic pedantry rather than essentially practical advice. Written in a mannered literary style, bristling with poetic imagery, the *Yuan ye* nevertheless stresses the importance of the major elements in a garden: water, rocks and buildings, mentioning plants mainly in relation to these and offering no advice on how to tend them.

The essential natural elements for a garden, water and rocks, were widely available. Water, which often formed the central focus of a garden, was plentiful in the rice-growing Yangtse Delta. In most gardens, if there was no spring within the grounds, local water sources were used, with canals leading water into the garden where it was collected into streams and pools [77, 78]. As the land is flat, there were no natural waterfalls but in the Shi zi lin (Grove of Stone Lions) in Suzhou, a reservoir for collecting rainwater was constructed above the Pavilion for Questioning the Plum and the accumulated water flowed down a series

75 Garden activities included painting, poetry writing, fishing, thinking and aggressive drinking games intended to make others drunk. From Xia Xianggeng's Shao you yuan er shi si xiao zhao tu (Twenty-four pictures of Wu Xinfu's 'Almost non-existent' garden), 1815. [15323 b. 15, ff. 40–41]

76 Theatrical scenes on a terrace with rocks, plum and banana beyond. From Wu Cheng'en's Xi xiang ji (Journey to the West), an 18th-century woodblock edition. [15271 c. 13]

of stone steps. Water was either 'assembled' in pools or 'dispersed', alternately revealed and hidden by rocks. In the former style, an open pool forms the centre of a garden (as in the Wang shi yuan, Garden of the Master of the Fishing Nets). 'Assembled' water could be 'divided' by creating an artificial impression of a distant source through the construction of a rocky ravine in a corner or adding a bridge. In the small private gardens, it was rare to find a bridge cutting across the centre of a pool for this could have contradicted the desired impression of open space. Low bridges, often of flat stones set at angles to form a zig-zag, cut across the corner of pools. For the same reason, and because open water was

77 *Wine and conversation by the water. Two gentlemen beside a lotus pond are attended by small servants bearing a jar of wine and a basket of cakes. From Xia Xianggeng's* Shao you yuan er shi si xiao zhao tu *(Twenty-four pictures of Wu Xinfu's 'Almost non-existent' garden), 1815. [15323 b. 15, p. 42]*

valued for its reflective qualities, it was rare to find water-lilies or lotuses covering a pool; they were restricted to the outer edges and carefully controlled. An open stretch of water allowed glimpses of the gold and silver carp, reflections of scudding clouds and the play of wind and rain on the clear surface. Great attention was paid to the banks of a pool which were ideally built up whilst retaining a 'natural' appearance. Earth banks seem to have been preferred during the Ming, but as they were susceptible to rain damage, they were gradually replaced by banks of piled rocks. Creeping plants such as wistaria or small trees were planted in crevices in the rocks and attention was paid to creating a natural descent from a rocky peak down to flatter stones nearer the surface of the water. Some buildings, usually the open pavilions known as 'dry boats', were built directly beside and slightly over the water and surrounded by marble balustrades.

In other gardens, rocks, rather than water, formed the main focus. Emperors like the Honourable Emperor of the Song reflected the passion for collecting strangely shaped rocks, many of which came, if not from further south, from the Yangtse Delta. Limestone rocks, pitted by the action of pebbles in the great lake at Wuxi, were amongst the favourites. They were artificially created, left in the lake for decades and the length of time they took to form added enormously to their price. Single rocks were set in courtyards or in front of halls and where no single rock of sufficient interest could be found, smaller rocks were piled into 'mock

78 Cooling down in the Lotus Pavilion, an open, breezy kiosk to be used in midsummer when the lotuses flowered. From Hong xue yin yuan, *the illustrated autobiography of Linqing.* [15292. f. 1/4]

*79 Paying a visit to the
flowers in the Wang garden,
a famous garden in Jiangsu
province. The dramatic
natural surroundings
contrast with the formal
courtyard groupings and
miniature mountains. From
Hong xue yin yuan, the
illustrated autobiography of
Linqing. [15292, f. 1/5]*

mountains' which towered over streams and could be ascended by
twisting stepped paths [79, 80]. The construction of 'mountains' was a
specialist art: the Lu family of Hangzhou 'piled up mountain peaks and
dug ravines with a skill that rivalled Heaven's'. There were differing
views on methods of construction although the aim was always realism.
Li Yu of the Qing wrote in his *Random notes of an idler*, 'After a lifetime of
travel and seeing all the famous gardens, I have never seen a mountain
which does not bear the marks of joints, chipping or drilling but which,
viewed from a distance, does not look like a real mountain'.[8] Some filled
in the gaps with earth, planted with creepers or trees, others preferred to
leave the stones bare. One of the great rock-piling experts of the Qing,
Zhang Lian, felt that the best method was to start with an earth mound
and cover that with mountains. The similarity of these mock mountains
to the imaginative peaks of Chinese landscape painting was emphasised by the involvement of artists in their design and the fact that they
were usually constructed on the basis of a drawing and a model made of

8 Edward Schaeffer, *The Vermilion
Bird* (Berkeley, University of
California Press, 1967).

clay and sand. Wooden piling was sometimes used as a foundation and iron nails, glutinous rice paste and plaster used to join rocks. Though Li Yu claimed that joints were always visible, care was taken to try and conceal methods of construction: when joining yellow limestone rocks, a mixture of iron filings and dark yellow clay from Yixing was used to ensure colour blending. Sometimes the mountains contained grottoes which could serve as rooms, cool in the heat of summer. Particularly where a distant view of a lake or pagoda was possible, tiny pavilions were sometimes placed on top of the 'mountain'. They had to be small, like the tiny Snail Shell pavilion, seven feet in diameter, in the Yi yuan (Suitable Garden) in Suzhou, to complete, rather than dominate, the mountain.

Buildings were the third major element in southern gardens. The house to which the garden was attached, usually took up about half the available space whilst, within the gardens, the proportion of space occupied by further buildings ranged between 30 per cent in small to medium-sized gardens and 15 per cent in the larger gardens where greater expanses of water and mountain were possible. Buildings, as one

80 A lady meets her lover by climbing up an artificial mountain and over a garden wall, from the novel Jin ping mei *(Plum in a golden vase). From a 1933 reprint of a woodblock edition with a preface dated 1617. [15334. b. 12]*

96

81

81 A young boy learns to read in a whitewashed garden schoolroom, with bamboo growing against the outer walls: furniture of twisted vine-roots and lattice windows complete the rustic effect. From Xia Xianggeng's Shao yu yuan er shi si xiao zhao tu *(Twenty-four pictures of Wu Xinfu's 'Almost non-existent' garden), 1815.* [15323 b. 15, ff. 2–3]

82 Listening to the evening rain on the banana leaves. Banana trees were frequently planted in South China not only for their fruit, but also for their quality of pluvial resonance. From Xia Xianggeng's Shao yu yuan er shi si xiao zhao tu *(Twenty-four pictures of Wu Xinfu's 'Almost non-existent' garden), 1815.* [15323 b. 15, ff. 6–7]

9 Liu Dunzhen, 'The Traditional Gardens of Suzhou' in *Garden History*, vol. 10, no. 2, 1982, pp. 108–141.

contemporary expert notes, 'provide places from which views can be admired', 'the means by which spaces are divided'[9] and also provide colour with their white-washed walls, grey tiles and dark chestnut timberwork [81, 82, 83]. In the last aspect, they have a close relationship with plants, for the form of bamboo is reflected and enhanced when it is set against a white wall and the whitewash means that plants can gain from reflected light. Halls of all sorts, 'dry boat' verandahed buildings over water, pavilions perched on mountain tops, are all light in construction since the climate of the Yangtse Delta is warm and it is in these garden buildings that the rather exaggerated upturned eaves of southern Chinese buildings are most often seen. Most of the buildings have façades of removable timber lattice panels that can be thrown open or taken out to reveal the garden, or closed so that greenery and rocks are glimpsed through the intricate lattice. Covered walks are also widely used to divide the garden, the walls often pierced with 'flower brick' openings of fanciful shapes – in the form of fans, leaves or plum flowers. As the visitor walks past, these decorative openings offer a glimpse of what lies beyond, like the slow unrolling of a handscroll landscape painting.

In a reverse of the western garden scheme, plants tend to be described last of all in Chinese works on gardens. Two major points were the preservation of large old trees, even when remodelling a garden, and all-year colour from the flowers of the four seasons. Magnolia and peonies were favoured in spring, wistaria, roses and lotuses in summer, chrysanthemum and maple trees in autumn and camellias, *Chimonanthus*

82

83

fragrans, the evergreen bamboo and early flowering prunus in winter. Some of these plants, such as roses and peonies, were best grown in raised beds with carved stone surrounds [85] and others, like chrysanthemum, were often raised in pots and brought out onto verandahs when they flowered [84, 86]. Other 'movable' plants were the small shrubs and trees grown in pots, their roots cut and their stems twisted to form miniatures. The technique, which originated in China where it is known as *pen cai* ('reared in pots') is better known in the west by the Japanese translation, *bonsai*. There is a related form in China known as *pen jing* or 'pot scene' where tiny mountain peaks (pieces of limestone or other rocks collected from famous lakes or mountains) were set in water in flattish earthenware dishes. The tiny peaks were often planted with moss, ferns and tiny saplings and sometimes further decorated with miniature clay pagodas, pavilions or bridges. They were known from the Mongol Yuan dynasty (1279–1368), when they were called little seed scenes, and they may well be older than that. Ming works on the history of Suzhou make it clear that they were a speciality of the area. *Pen jing*, *pen cai* and potted plants were often displayed on stone tables set against the white-washed walls of side courtyards. Though deer were too big for the small southern gardens, bright gold and silver carp were often raised in pools and songbirds in elaborate bamboo cages were brought into the garden to sing (and Manchu aristocrats buried their pet dogs in the grounds of their mansions).

The importance of dividing up even a small garden to provide a series of separate views was fundamental to the plan. Gardens were ideally

83 Supervising the airing of the library: note the potted epidendrum on a stand and the cross-shaped opening framing the bamboo clump. From Xia Xianggeng's Shao yu yuan er shi si xiao zhao tu *(Twenty-four pictures of Wu Xinfu's 'Almost non-existent' garden), 1815. [15323 b. 15, ff. 4–5]*

approached by a narrow twisting path to increase the visitor's anticipation; a method successfully used in the public approach to the Wang shi yuan (Master of the Nets) garden in Suzhou which is, today, approached by the former rear gate. Alternatively, as in *Hong Lou Meng* (the 'Dream of the Red Chamber'), the first scene of a garden was tantalizingly glimpsed through the lattice screens of a gatehouse. Each hall or pavilion had its own 'view', of a pool, mountain or spectacular plant. Side courtyards were sometimes paved with differently coloured pebbles forming tiny pictures of vases of flowers, deer or auspicious designs such as interlocked coins. Bamboos were planted against the whitewashed walls and the central focus of such a courtyard might be a single lake rock or a raised bed of carved stone filled with peonies or roses.

Though the gardens of the Yangtse Delta represented the highest form of traditional garden design, the love of gardens, plants and flowers was not restricted to the south. In North China, where the climate is not conducive to all-year gardening, garden buildings were often painted. In the city of Ji'nan in Shandong province where there are many natural springs, one garden makes use of the constantly moving water as a major focus, viewed from an open pavilion with bright red timberwork and yellow glazed tiles, colourful even on a grey winter day. The same use of brightly coloured painted decoration can be seen in the Yi he yuan Summer Palace outside Peking where even in the Garden of Harmonious Interest, modelled on a southern garden, all the buildings have columns painted red and horizontal rafters painted with multi-coloured landscape scenes. Trees were traditionally planted in the tiny courtyards of ordinary houses in Peking so that 19th century western travellers who viewed the city from its high walls described it as 'a great wood' or *rus in urbe*. Trees or vines grown over a trellis (and carefully protected under straw and clay during the freezing winter) provided summer shade and, since other plants could not be left out all year, some Peking residents set aside one room to over-winter plants, keeping it warm and covering the walls with oiled paper to reduce pests. When the weather allowed, flowering oleanders, single lotus flowers in large pots, fragrant osmanthus, hibiscus and other potted plants were set out in the courtyard, alongside large ceramic jars full of precious goldfish, black, silver and gold.

84 The Qing official Linqing kept editions of his mother's poems in his 'Half Acre garden'. Wisteria frames the windows which have bamboo roller blinds for summer and potted plants stand in the courtyard. From Hong xue yin yuan, *the illustrated autobiography of Linqing.* [15292, f. 1/5]

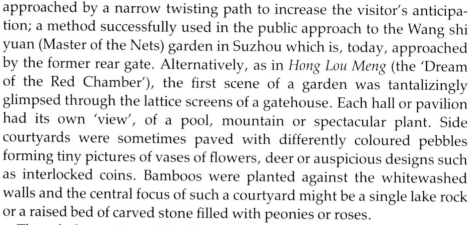

85

85 *Watering the flowers in raised stone beds. The 'half' pavilion by the wall has a tromp-l'oeil stone-carved landscape and elegant seats with swan's neck backs. From Xia Xianggeng's* Shao yu yuan er shi si xiao zhao tu *(Twenty-four pictures of Wu Xinfu's 'Almost non-existent' garden), 1815.*
[15323 b. 15, ff. 44–45]

86 *Ladies in a garden with a climbing plant grown over a frame, potted orchids and a 'pot scene' in the centre background. From a Ming illustrated work included in* Zhong guo ban hua xuan *(Selection of Chinese woodblock illustrations), 1958.*
[15530 b. 67, vol. 2, pl. 96]

Japan

87 Ladies in a house, with blinds rolled up to reveal the adjoining garden, from a Japanese manuscript of Yurikawa Daijan, *a tale about a warrior. Colours painted on paper, 17th–18th century. [Or. 13822]*

From the fifth century AD, Japanese gardens were strongly influenced by their Chinese neighbour's parks and planting. Four years after the first Japanese embassy to China, led by Ono no Imoko in 607, the first landscaped garden with a lake was recorded as being constructed in the imperial palace in the capital of Nara (near Kyoto). It would appear that some of the features of this garden were built by a Korean craftsman known as the 'Ugly artisan' because the skin of his face was spotted with white. He built a bridge across the lake, assumed to be a high-arched red-painted bridge in the contemporary Chinese style, and a 'mountain'.

Little is known about the latter structure, though one expert considers that it may have been a sort of fountain made out of a pile of hollow stones that could be filled with water which spouted out through small openings in one of the lower stones. Some suggest that this was a representation of Sumeru, the mountain at the centre of the nine mountains in the Buddhist plan of the universe; thus this early garden anticipates a later form based on temple gardens constructed to represent an earthly version of the Buddhist paradise as described in the *Lotus sutra*. Early Japanese literary accounts describe such mountain fountains as dating back to the Chinese Han dynasty, though they no longer survive in China, and so this example represents the first survival in Japan of garden elements long lost in China.

In this early period, the word that the Japanese used for a garden was *shima* which meant island, firmly establishing a connection with the early Chinese imperial gardens dominated by a lake with islands of the

immortals. Contemporary Chinese garden styles were also reflected in some of the contents of the imperial treasure-house Shōsōin where an eighth-century painted screen depicts a lady sitting on a pitted lake rock beside a tree with a picturesquely twisted trunk. There was also a form of *pen jing* (pot scene) in the collection, made entirely from wood carved to represent a mountainous island, its cliffs cut away by the action of water. Though almost nothing survives of the gardens of Nara, fragmentary references can be gathered from poems of the period which include mention of flowering plants, lakes, willows and plum trees and pleasure boats.

Early in the Heian period (794–1185), an imperial park was laid out with a lake filled by a spring and dotted with islands in the Chinese imperial style. Willows bordered the paths and a large pavilion overlooked the lake. As befitted an imperial park modelled on those of the Chinese emperors, it was used by the court for banquets, boating and sporting events. Another garden, which represents a rare survival, was the Saga-no-in where the Emperor Saga retired in 823. His lake, bordered by cherry and maples, once had a string of five linked 'islands' of rock set in a carefully prepared lake whose floor was paved with pebbles set in clay. A 'cascade' on the north bank of the pool is of considerable interest. Now dry, it has been studied by garden historians who think that it may well have always been dry. Such 'dry waterfalls' became a characteristic feature of later Japanese gardens, made from carefully piled rocks which looked like those over which water tumbled naturally. These were sometimes selected for their patterns, with light stripes suggesting falling water. Ostensibly very much part of later Japanese gardens (distanced from those of the more literally-minded Chinese), the presence of a dry waterfall in the Emperor Saga's garden does suggest a Chinese prototype for he was a passionate devotee of all things Chinese.[1] This is particularly interesting, both since no such dry waterfalls survive in Chinese gardens, and in view of the rather different development of later Japanese and Chinese gardens. The Chinese generally eschewed such devices in favour of real lakes, ponds, streams and cascades, whilst Japan became famous for its metaphorical temple gardens where sand and rocks substituted for mountains and lakes.

A detailed description of a Chinese garden was given in the 18th-century novel *Heng Lou Meng* (the 'Dream of the Red Chamber'), but a group of Japanese works of literature, best exemplified by Lady Murasaki's 'Tale of Genji'[2] (late 10th century) give a much earlier view of courtly gardens. Each of the ladies wooed by Prince Genji lived in a separate estate where a garden was a major feature. For one, he made an autumn garden full of trees whose leaves turned deepest red before they fell and where boulders were set in a stream to increase the dramatic sound of

1 Loraine Kuck, *The world of the Japanese garden* (New York and Tokyo, Walker/Weatherhill, 1968).

2 Murasaki Shikibu, *The Tale of Genji*, translated by E. Seidensticker (London, Secker and Warburg, 1976).

88

89

water crashing through rocks. Another lady was favoured with a winter garden with a bed of chrysanthemum (for the early winter) and many pine-trees which she could admire when laden with snow. By contrast, a summer garden (for yet another of Genji's consorts) contained scented flowers, peonies, roses and orange blossom as well as shady plants: bamboos and tall forest trees formed cool green tunnels around the spring and pool. Lady Murasaki's garden was at its best in spring when its hillside cherry orchards flowered like white clouds and the fresh yellow-green leaves of willows swept the courtyard. She had wistaria and mountain kerria, the former softly draped over doorways and covered walks, the kerria tumbling down over the 'cliffs' that had been cunningly made on the banks of the lake. Such differentiated gardens were quite easily accommodated in the rambling homes of Heian aristocrats. These were made up of a series of buildings, usually connected by covered walks which led the way through landscaped gardens. Manuscript and woodblock illustrations to the great Japanese novels such as 'The Tale of Genji' invariably depict the 'edges' of houses [see 90], the raised verandah, the paper screen walls and the stepping stones, bamboos, streams and twisted pines of the garden beyond [88].

88 A duet between a gentleman playing the flute in a garden and his lady inside on the koto. From Genji Monogatari (The tale of Genji), *woodblock print, 1650.*
[16055 b. 1, vol. 2, p. 23]

89 Accompanied by his servant, a gentleman departs through a garden at dawn. Cockerels and chickens roost in the willow beside a rustic fence. From Ise Monogatari (The tale of Ise), *1610.*
[Or. 65 c. 1]

90 The serenity of spring: the edge of a verandah and a garden with scattered petals and rocks. From Ogawa Ritsuo, Chichi no on, *a haiku anthology. Japanese coloured woodblock, 1730. [Or. 74 cc. 3]*

91 The courtyard of the Shounji (Temple of the Beneficent Clouds), where the central focus is an ancient five-leaved pine, propped up amongst rocks and viewed from the verandah. From Akisato Shosen, Izumi meisho zue (Views in Izumi province), *woodblock print, 1796. [16114 d. 1]*

92 A lotus pool in a naturalistic temple garden in the Nanzenji, Kyoto. From Akisato Rito, Miyako insen meisho zue (Illustrated guide to Kyoto), *1799. [16114 d. 10]*

Princes creep through the garden to visit their lovers, incongruously (given the ostensible secrecy of the event) attended by small servants [89]; they leave billets-doux written on slips of paper folded into origami shapes and pushed under the screen. Ladies, their long hair flowing in waves, seem to wait eternally behind screens, peeping out at the garden below.

Such detailed literary accounts of gardens and their habitués indicate a particular love of brightly-coloured flowers in the Heian period. Though flowering plants were still used with great skill, many later Japanese gardens were more sombre, dominated by the greens of moss, bamboo and pines set off by dark rocks and light sand. In the Kamakura period (1185–1333), larger gardens were constructed with winding pools and hillside walks, in contrast with the enclosures of the Heian era. Even the pools were differently used. During the Heian period, lakes were specifically designed to be viewed from pleasure boats. Many of the rock mountains set in the lakes presented a fine view from the main pavilion but were also designed with coves and cliffs to the rear, visible only from a boat.

The Kamakura era also saw the construction of great temple gardens [91, 92]. Their Chinese antecedents have not survived: the eighth century imperial suppression of Buddhism in China was largely a response to the

91

92

*93 Recommended gardening
tools and a method of moving
large rocks with a windlass.
From Kitamara Enkin,
Chikuzan teizoden (How
to make mountains and
gardens), woodblock print,
1795. [16003 b. 13, garden
section part 2, p. 17]*

*94 Sieve, trowels, mattocks,
mallets and other tools, from
Chikuzan reizoden (How
to make mountains and
gardens). [16003 b. 13,
garden section, part 2, p. 18]*

*95 The raked garden of the
Daitokuji in Kyoto, from
Akisato Rito, Miyako rinsen
meisho zue (Illustrated
guide to Kyoto), 1799.
[16114 d. 10]*

*96 How to construct a
realistic mountain with
numbered stones and trees,
from Chikuzan reizoden
(How to make mountains and
gardens), woodblock print,
1795. [16003 b. 13, garden
section part 1, f. 8]*

growing economic power of the Buddhist church and the vast estates of
the temples were confiscated so that whilst Chinese Buddhist monks and
nuns continue to cultivate flowers and grow vegetables, they now do so
in the restricted space of temple courtyards and tiny garden plots. In
Japan, by contrast, temple gardens are amongst the most famous in the
country and, together with surviving aristocratic gardens and tea-house
gardens, remain major monuments.

The first surviving Japanese garden manual, a manuscript by Tachibana
no Toshitsuna, the *Sakuteiki* (Notes on making gardens) dates from the
Kamakura period. This and the 15th-century manuscript, *Senzui narabi ni
yagyō no zu* (Illustrated designs for mountain, water and hill landscapes)
by the Buddhist priest Zōen, form the basic early literature on garden
construction, antedating surviving Chinese texts. It seems likely that
texts were of more significance in Japanese garden design than in
Chinese. Production of such textbooks continued into the Edo period
(1615–1868) when the very detailed *Tsukiyama teizōden* (Creating landscape gardens) was published which includes details of the types of
trowels, hatchets and pruners to be used and illustrations of how to
move large rocks on rollers using a windlass and pry bars [93, 94]. During
the Edo period, a number of guidebooks to major gardens, especially
those of the temples in the Kyoto area, also appeared, to aid tourists and
inspire designers [95]. Another major Edo gardening manual, *Ishigumi
sono yaegaki den* (Illustrated work on landscape gardening) contained
numerous illustrations, particularly of small tea-house gardens, illustrating an enormous variety of exceedingly similar designs, subtly differentiated by the disposition of the same elements: stepping stones, bridges,
streams, marsh plants, lanterns, rocks and small trees [96].

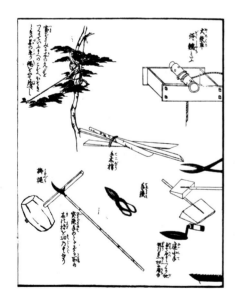
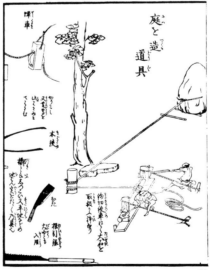
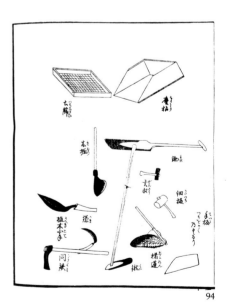

93

94

The *Sakuteiki* was written by an aristocrat who was clearly personally involved in the practicalities of garden building, recalling Prince Genji who himself rolled up his sleeves and directed the workmen as they toiled over rock-moving. In that sense, the text is similar to that of the later Chinese 'Craft of Gardens' which was also written by a man with practical experience, despite his constant literary allusions. The first principle established in the *Sakuteiki* was the importance of visiting famous sites of natural beauty, to absorb the principles of natural design. Copying natural scenes became an important aspect of the aristocratic gardens of Japan and included the very beautiful coastline as well as mountain sites. In the Korakuen imperial park near Tokyo, laid out on the orders of the shogun Tokugawa Yorifusa (1603–61), 30 famous sites in Japan were copied and, later, some famous Chinese views were also

97 A lonely and romantic young man in a mosquito net with a stream and watercourse outside in the garden. Illustration by Sekkosai in Shinobu-zuri *(Recollections prints), Japanese stencil colour print, Kyoto, 1750. [Or. 81. c. 27]*

added in miniature. One of the most attractive reproductions is the copy of the coastal sandbar at Amanohashidate in the 17th-century Katsura imperial villa near Kyoto. The garden version is more winding than the original and covered with twisted pines imitating the wind-blown trees of the coast.

The major section of the *Sakuteiki* deals with the creation of 'mountain streams' which should ideally develop from a rivulet rushing through a deep gully to a broader, eddying stream flowing into a pond. The disposition of rocks and trees was also of paramount importance. Zōen's 'illustrated designs' show exactly how rocks should be placed in different contexts. There are boat-concealing rocks in an otherwise open pool (reflecting the Heian love of boat trips) and there are named groupings of stones. One of the most famous is the 'Buddhist triad' where three stones, the largest at the centre, imitate the trinity of Buddhist images in Buddhist temples. This type of detail is lacking in later Chinese texts and

98 A coloured woodblock depiction of a house in rustic surroundings, from Bumpo Basei, Teito gakei ichiran *(Sketches of the neighbourhood of Kyoto), Kyoto 1809–1816. [16112 d. 14, Book 4]*

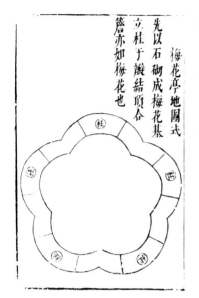

99 Plan of a pavilion in the form of a plum blossom. From Ji Cheng's Yuan Ye (Craft of gardens), reprint of a 1635 woodblock edition in a Japanese collection. [15305 e. 14]

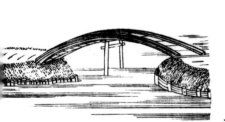

3 David A. Slawson, Secret teachings in the art of Japanese gardens (Tokyo and New York, Kodansha, 1987).

4 Ji Cheng, The Craft of Gardens, translated by Alison Hardie (New Haven and London, Yale University Press, 1988).

indicates the diverging aesthetic. The Chinese liked stones that looked like things – oxen, lions and cranes – but the Japanese were more concerned with form than appearance. Zōen's illustrations of trees include many described in terms of their line and in illustrations depicting rocks already in position, he notes exactly what sort of tree should be planted where [100]. This absolute attention to concrete detail was an important aspect of training apprentices and contrasts with the air of mystery that grew up around the acquisition of knowledge. The early texts on gardens were described as 'secret texts' transmitting only part of the esoteric skill of garden design. Students in Japan today still have to serve a long apprenticeship of three to five years spent weeding and pruning whilst they assimilate the secret skills of their master through 'body learning' (learning by doing). Then they may be allowed access to the texts which themselves contain injunctions against widespread transmission: 'the illustrations concerning rocks . . . must be kept quite secret'.[3] Secrecy was not part of the Chinese tradition and though the language of Ji Cheng's 'Craft of Gardens' may seem occasionally unhelpful ('There is no set formula for pavilions, nor any rule for their disposition'),[4] there is no danger attached to its content and it was published for the discerning and would-be fashionable gentlemen of 17th-century China. The only remotely similar prohibitions can be found in the Chinese carpenters' 'bible', 'The Classic of Lu Ban', which was a rather different sort of text since it included a large number of spells and talismans to protect (or destroy) buildings.

The twists and turns of Japanese history particularly in the 13th to 15th centuries saw the development of new forms of garden alongside the old. Imperial and aristocratic villas built on large mountain sites permitted the continuing use of a garden form quite close to the Chinese prototypes of the Tang dynasty. These were the 'stroll gardens' where visitors were encouraged to range around the lake or traverse it by boat to see the different set-pieces from a variety of angles. The Eifukuji, laid out in Kamakura by the monk Jogen for Minamoto Yorimoto in 1189, was based on the Fujiwara temple of Mōtsuji which Yorimoto had seen when he led his army against the Fujiwara stronghold. A stream was led down to the lake through banks lined by stones and the islands of the lake were linked by scarlet bridges. In the lake itself were groups of rocks known as the 'night-mooring islands' and tortoise island (this latter a rare but popularly used form of a group of stones arranged to look like a tortoise). Such grand imperial parks continued to be constructed, especially with a new vogue for Chinese styles that prevailed in the 14th and 15th centuries. The 'Gold Pavilion' near Kyoto was a version of a Chinese lake-side pavilion and was constructed in 1395 for the Ashigaka shogun Yoshimitsu when he retired. In the Gold Pavilion, he would drink tea

草之築山之全圖

100 How to make a grassy slope, using numbered stones, from Kitamura Enkin, Chikuzan teizoden *(How to make mountains and gardens), woodblock print, 1795 [16033 d. 17, garden section, part 1, p. 17]*

brewed from spring water, another innovation introduced from China. The lake beside the pavilion was not meant to be 'strolled round'; its islands and rocks were supposed to be viewed from boats. The rocky groups included a 'tortoise island' like that in the Eifukuji, made of a cluster of stones resembling the shell, head and flippers of a turtle. The association of turtles with longevity probably contributed to their representation in stone and another island in the lake was called the crane island, for cranes were also associated with long life in Chinese and Japanese myth. The crane islands differed from tortoise islands in that they rarely looked much like cranes but consisted of a tall, narrow rock, merely hinting at a long-necked bird peering out over the water. Yoshimitsu continued to improve his garden, particularly with new rocks that were presented to him by his vassals. One, which arrived in 1229, required the strength of 17 oxen to move it. In his acceptance of 'tribute' rocks and use of manpower, Yoshimitsu was no different from other shoguns who constructed their gardens on an appropriately grand scale. Records of such efforts include the use of 1,800 men to move a couple of rocks a few miles, and the suicide of two gardeners when a branch was broken off a plum tree in transit.

101 Different types of garden bridge: rustic, grass-bordered and with a sudden drop at one end to stepping stones below (above) or a smooth curve (opposite). From Akisato Rito's Ishigumi sono yaekiden *(Eight methods of piling rocks to create a garden), woodblock print, c.1827. [16033 a. 12, part 1, pp. 28–9]*

102

102 How to make a stone garden: raked sand between the stones, with a single pine beyond. From Kitamura Enkin, Chikusan teizoden (How to make mountains and gardens), woodblock print, 1795. [16033 d. 17, garden section, part 3, p. 33]

103 Varying forms of rustic fencing for tea-house gardens from Ishigumi sono yaekiden (Eight methods of piling rocks to create a garden), woodblock print c.1827. [16033 a. 12, p. 13]

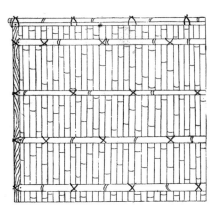

Yoshimitsu's grandson Yoshimasa built a 'Silver Pavilion' in 1482, one of twelve major timber structures in a large hill-side 'stroll garden' near Kyoto. These included a main gate, covered walks, a study, a hump-backed bridge and several pavilions with specific uses: one was for watching football (a game played by long-gowned gentlemen in Song dynasty China and, subsequently, Japan), others for religious cere-monies or tea-drinking. A cascade, called the Moon-washing Spring, fell into the Brocade Mirror Pool and the best view of the garden and the rising moon was from the Silver Pavilion. Yoshimasa's garden, and the later Katsura villa with its lake, bridges, islands, football pitch and other sporting areas, were quite close to Chinese originals but one feature, possibly an accidental survival of the restoration of the Silver Pavilion in 1615, ostensibly associates the Pavilion with the rise of the unique temple gardens. The most extraordinary features of the Silver Pavilion park today are two sand piles. A large cut-off cone of silvery sand is now named the 'moon-facing eminence' and, beside it, a flat, terrace-like pile is known as the 'silver sand sea'. It seems likely that silver sand was used to cover the ground before the pavilion (sand had been used in this way since the Heian period) and that these now sculptured heaps do not represent Zen constructions but were simply the result of building works, subsequently frozen in time and venerated.

Whatever the origin of the 'moon-facing eminence', the raked sand gardens found in Zen temples in Japan are amongst the most remarkable

謝酌吳姬倒一
樽醉暗香不
嫌春夜冷逢月
照新妝
翠春雄

104 *Wine and books on a spring evening beneath the prunus. From* Chikudo gafu *(Drawing book of Chikudo), a coloured woodblock print, 1815. [16116 b. 25]*

'gardens' in the world [102]. Small in scale, no bigger than a tennis court, intended to form the main view from a Zen abbot's living room, they indicate the enormous influence that Zen Buddhism had on Japanese garden design. Better known by its Japanese name, Zen, the Chan or 'meditation' school developed in China, partly as a means for lay persons to achieve enlightenment without necessarily leaving home (and abandoning parents and ancestors) and entering a monastery. In Japan, it remained somewhat different from the other sects (its abbots were allowed to marry, for example), though it developed into more of a monastic tradition than it had been in China. The fundamental belief in meditation became associated with practices or 'ways' to achieve the goal of enlightenment and these included the 'way of tea', the 'way of flowers', the 'way of archery'. These 'ways' led to a great elevation of

105

105 Different types of garden lantern, From Kitamura Enkin, Chikuzan teizoden (How to make mountains and gardens), woodblock print, 1795. [16033 d. 17, garden section, part 2, p. 34]

106 Wash basin beside a tea-house, from Chikuzan teizoden (How to make mountains and gardens), 1795. [16033 d. 17, garden section, part 2, p. 26]

107 The disposition of rocks and trees, each carefully labelled so that exactly the same form can be achieved. From Akisato Rito's Ishigumi sono yaekiden (Eight methods of piling rocks to create a garden), woodblock print. c.1827. [16033 a. 12, part 2, f. 16]

aesthetics, infused by the austerity of Zen. The metaphysical practice of Zen meditation contributed to the development of metaphysical gardening; moss gardens (bare of flowers), 'dry' waterfalls and streams, rocks and swept sand instead of seas and islands, all these were associated with Zen. Austerity and esotericism mingled in Zen gardens. Mossy slopes were kept meticulously free of fallen leaves and other debris, yet one layman who swept a moss garden too assiduously was silently reproved by his abbot who gently shook the branches of a maple in autumn, scattering a few choice red leaves on a green bed.

Perhaps the first 'Zen' garden is the 13th-century Saihōji or Moss temple near Kyoto. This combines a lower garden in the more traditional Chinese-influenced style with an unusual 'stroll garden' in the upper forest. There, a dry cascade of stepped rocks falls from a woodland 'spring' filled with moss, not water, surrounded by low 'kneeling stones'. Later Zen gardens, typified by the small walled enclosures set outside the abbots' living quarters, no longer used the 'stroll garden' principle but were intended to be viewed from a single position, on the verandah outside the main room. Though this single viewpoint plan was widely used in Chinese gardens (in the side courtyards of southern houses) and also during the Heian period, it was developed to a high point in Zen temples. Below the raised verandah in the Daisen'in (part of the Daitokuji temple in Tokyo) is an area of carefully raked sand, striped, piled in island cones. Rocks are arranged to the side and rear of the raked sand; a 'dry' waterfall, a dry 'boat' with a few tiny shrubs planted on and among them. In the late 15th century Ryōanji, the barest of all, five groups of rocks stand in a raked sand sea. The area (the size of a tennis court) is walled and elegantly surrounded by a border of diamond-patterned flagstones and a channel of dark pebbles bordered by paler stones. Above the dark, tiled wall opposite the verandah rise tall green trees.

The smallness of these temple courtyard gardens, as well as the Zen elevation of tea-drinking to an art form with religious connotations, may have contributed to the development of the tea-house garden [*see* 103, 104]. Like the house-garden complexes of south China, where house and garden form a unity, the tiny rustic thatched cottages used for the tea ceremony in Japan were invariably set in a tiny garden courtyard. One authority calls the tea-house garden a 'garden path' for it is a route along which the visitor travels, shedding the cares of the world as he prepares himself for the cleansing ceremony. That it is a route is emphasised by the carefully laid stepping stones or pebbled paths that lead him to the tea-house, through clumps of bamboo, past rock groupings and low shrubs and tiny trees, his way illuminated by stone lanterns [105]. These, consisting of tall stone stems topped by cut-out stones that often resemble small roofed pavilions, probably derive from Tang dynasty Chinese models, though many were imported from Korea. Beside the tea-house is a large stone, either a natural stone with a depression in its upper surface or a specially carved stone, filled with water and provided with a simple bamboo dipper for the visitor to wash his hands [106].

108 A suggested design for a suburban tea-house from Chikuzan teizoden (*How to make mountains and gardens*), *1795. [16033 d. 17, garden section part 1, p. 34]*

In the tea-house enclosure, whether a free-standing structure or one of many set in an imperial park, flowers were kept to a minimum, for this is one of the most pared-down 'aesthetic' forms of the Japanese garden [107, 108]. Ferns were planted beside rocks but, at most, only a prunus (for its sparse, elegant flowers in the early spring) or a small-leafed maple (acceptable as a native tree) could be included. Though flowers were thus excluded from the tea-house, in other parts of a large garden, just as in Chinese gardens, flowers could provide a focus. Like the Chinese, the Japanese enjoy the flowers of the seasons, making special trips to gardens famous for a particular flowering plant at the appropriate season. The late winter flowers and plants are the same in China and

109 Pot plants (three varieties of Nandina domestica *by Untei). From* Somoku Kihin Kagami *(Mirror of rare plants and trees), Japanese hand-coloured woodblock, 1827.*
[16033 c. 3]

Japan: evergreen bamboo and pine which, together with the early-flowering plum, are known as the 'three friends of winter'. Prunus blossoms are known in Japan as 'snow flowers' for their sparse, snowflake-like scatter amongst dark branches, as well as the fact that it often snows as they flower [see 112]. One of the great winter flowers, the camellia, native to East Asia, was only planted in Buddhist temples, for the sudden dropping of the red flower at its peak was regarded as ominous (death in the midst of life) to all but Buddhist monks whose life was spent in contemplation of this very notion. Just as in China, the first yellow buds on the willow were to be appreciated slightly later in spring as an indication of a real change in the season and, in mid-April, this is followed by the special Japanese favourite, cherry blossom [see 111]. Many of the great gardens of Kyoto, especially the Heian Shrine, specialize in cherry blossoms of all sorts, from the pink fountains of weeping cherries to the cloudlike orchards by the lake. Later came azaleas and wistaria. It is interesting that azaleas were particularly beloved of the Japanese and do not form part of the major seasonal

110 A bonsai establishment in 18th-century Edo (Tokyo). Coloured woodblock print from Ehon Toto meisho (Famous sights of Edo), c.1770. [16114 e. 93]

*111 Picnic at Cherry blossom
time in Omuro in Kyoto.
From* Miyako meisho zue
*(Illustrated guide to Kyoto),
1780. [16114 d. 11]*

flowerings in their native country, China, though the wistaria was
appreciated in both countries. In Japan, the waterside iris was the
dominant flower of summer, seen at its best in the Meiji Shrine in Tokyo.
Clumps of *Iris kaempferi* are planted in a winding stream, crossed by a low
rustic bridge, and set against a background of Japanese maples whose
foliage in summer is a plain green foil for the purple iris. In late summer,
the morning glory is followed by the Japanese bush clover. Planted in
the sand-covered courts of buildings like the Seiryōden imperial palace in
Kyoto, the small shrubs are covered with pink blossoms in September
and are then cut down to ground level, to promote a bushy growth next
spring. Maples, planted on all the hillsides of large imperial parks and
sometimes used as a 'borrowed' view, to be admired from the verandah
of a hill-side temple surrounded by trees, were the sight of late autumn.
Then, when the irises of the Meiji shrine have finished flowering, their
'background' maples assume the foreground. Last of all comes the
chrysanthemum.

Pen cai, or *bonsai* in Japanese, the most highly developed Chinese form
of miniaturisation, were particularly popular from the 17th century and
have been made very much a Japanese art form, tiny, spiky and far
removed from the larger, more naturalistic Chinese originals [110].
Though a relatively late introduction, the same sort of lengthy apprenticeship and absorption of tradition specified for garden design was
applied to *bonsai*. 'It takes three years to learn to water a tree properly',[5]
as one handbook notes severely, before proceeding with instructions on
exactly which of the six different types of pruning scissors should be

5 Yuji Yoshimura and Giovanna
M. Halford, *The Japanese art of
miniature trees and landscapes*
(Rutland and Tokyo, Tuttle, 1957).

used on deciduous, as opposed to fruit-bearing, trees. In *bonsai* as in garden planning, a careful study of the natural origin was important. The best *bonsai* trees are pines and junipers which either originate, or look as if they originated, on a barren mountainside or wind-swept shore, their trunks and branches twisted by storms, their growth stunted by thin soils. After this poor start in life, the subject was ruthlessly pruned and wired and set in a 'training pot' in a mixture of fermented cottonseed, fishmeal, lime, soya beans and wood ash. Styles of training were many, and all were laid down. Sixteen types of single-trunk bonsai included 'coiled', 'windswept', 'twisted trunk', 'octopus' and 'clinging to a rock', whilst varied effects were achieved by teasing multiple trunks from a single root or group plantings of two or more saplings. These miniatures were made for individual display and appreciation and are a form quite separate from the fashion for dwarf garden trees which grew up at roughly the same time. Dwarf trees and shrubs in gardens were pruned to keep them in proportion with the garden. As Japan's towns and cities grew more crowded, private gardens were constrained. Where huge forests of pine and maple had been possible in the old imperial estates, the aesthetic of the tea-garden, combined with lack of space, forced a reduction in scale which was carried out with absolute precision.

112 Admiring the early flowering prunus on a riverbank in Kyoto at the Sainenji temple. From Miyako meisho zue (Illustrated guide to Kyoto), 1780.
[16114 d. 11]